QUEEN ELIZABETH II

TIMES BOOKS

Published by Times Books

An imprint of HarperCollins Publishers
Westerhill Road, Bishopbriggs
Glasgow G64 2QT

HarperCollins Publishers
1st Floor, Watermarque Building,
Ringsend Road, Dublin 4, Ireland

First edition 2021

A catalogue record for this book is available
from the British Library.

ISBN 978-0-00-848520-7

10 9 8 7 6 5 4 3 2 1

Printed in Bosnia and Herzegovina by GPS Group

Thanks and acknowledgements go to Lily Carlton,
Joanne Lovey and Robin Ashton at News Syndication
and, in particular, at The Times, Ian Brunskill and, at
HarperCollins, Rachel Allegro, Jethro Lennox,
Sonya Newland and Kevin Robbins.

This book is produced from independently certified
FSC™ paper to ensure responsible forest management.

For more information visit: www.harpercollins.co.uk/green

THE TIMES
QUEEN ELIZABETH II

A PORTRAIT OF HER 70-YEAR REIGN

Edited by

James Owen

CONTENTS

"I declare before you all that my whole life whether it be long or short shall be devoted to your service..."

The Queen, April 21, 1947

INTRODUCTION

by James Owen

There are few other presences in most people's lives as constant as the Queen. Britain's longest-reigning monarch has been our sovereign for 70 years and famous for almost 100. She is as much a part of our culture as red post boxes, as familiar as cloudy skies and as reassuring as tea and toast. And yet, what do we really know about her?

A century ago, when she was born, such a question would not have been asked. The press, like everyone else, knew their place. That of the royal family was at the top of society, indeed at the top of a world in which Britain, with an empire covering a quarter of the globe, was still the dominant power.

With ever-gathering speed, that world has changed forever during Elizabeth's reign. She has been at the centre of extraordinary events, not least in her own family, for decade after decade. And yet, she has weathered them.

More than most, she has had to adapt herself to a different way of doing things. The outer splendour of her life may have appeared to remain much the same, but during her years on the throne the monarchy has had to renegotiate its relationship with its subjects. It has had to accept far greater scrutiny of its privileges and much more curiosity about the behaviour of those who enjoy them.

The Queen, however, with very few exceptions, has never lost her standing with her people; it is impossible to think of her, unlike Queen Victoria, being booed in public. Always on show, never saying anything controversial – indeed hardly anything truly memorable – she has allowed few glimpses of what she actually thinks or feels.

She is simply there, and we are rightly grateful for her decades of unstinting service and for the stability she provides. But she is an enigma.

As we celebrate her Platinum Jubilee, as what were key moments in both her life and ours turn from news into history, this volume both preserves her remarkable achievements and seeks to understand how she came to accomplish them.

If the photographs provide a comprehensive record of her public life, the selection of short essays by writers at *The Times* and by leading royal historians, interspersed with contemporary news reports on turning points in her life, offer a series of perspectives on the less visible Queen – the private experiences and inner qualities that have shaped her and her reign.

Her path to the throne was extraordinary just in itself. When she was born, in 1926, there was no expectation that she would become Queen, as her father, then the Duke of York, was the younger brother of the heir, the future King Edward VIII. With her uncle's abdication in 1936, her world, and that of her parents and her sister, Princess Margaret, was turned upside down.

Like ordinary Britons, she endured the war years, served in the armed forces as a driver, and even escaped briefly from Buckingham Palace to take part in the jubilation of VE Day. Her choice of a husband was similarly bold, for Prince Philip was, by royal standards, an outsider, a foreigner, a refugee even, with few prospects and a maverick, modernising streak.

Nevertheless, he gave her the support she needed when she succeeded to the throne at 25, in 1952, and provided much of the impetus for the changes needed to fit the institution of monarchy to a new world. The essays detail the Queen's relationships with the prime ministers who have served her, beginning with Winston Churchill, her influence on diplomatic relations with countries such as America, and her dedicated leadership of a Commonwealth which now encompasses 54 different nations.

What has sustained her all these years, beyond her profound sense of duty, are her enthusiasms, notably horse racing and her beloved dogs, her homes, and her family – her parents, her children and now the grandchildren and great-grandchildren who will follow her.

Together with her shrewd choice of advisers, they have enabled her in the last 20 years to transform faster than ever the shape of the monarchy, recognising the public discontent that met the official reaction to the death of Diana, Princess of Wales, and rebuilding, too, from the ashes of the fire-ravaged Windsor Castle.

For all the pageantry and ceremony with which we associate the Queen in her public role, what has underpinned this is her personal modesty, the sense that she has never taken things for granted. We have been very fortunate to have her all these years. Long may she yet reign – happy and glorious!

The Queen at the Royal Windsor Cup, July 2021.

BORN
TO SERVE

⟨ Birth of a Princess ⟩

The Court Circular issued from Windsor Castle last night opens with the following paragraph: The King and Queen have received with great pleasure the news that the Duchess of York gave birth to a daughter this morning. Their Majesties had been awakened between 3 and 4 a.m. to receive the news of the birth of their first grand-daughter. No. 17, Bruton street, where the Duke and Duchess recently went to reside temporarily, is the London residence of the Earl and Countess of Strathmore, the parents of the Duchess of York, who had been staying in London in view of the expected birth of the child.

In accordance with custom where births in the royal family are concerned, the Home Secretary, Sir William Joynson-Hicks, had been summoned to Bruton street, and he was present in the house at the time of the birth. In accordance with custom also the Home Secretary conveyed to the Lord Mayor by special messenger the intimation of the birth of the Princess. The announcement and the subsequent bulletin were posted outside the Mansion House. To a telegram from the Mansion House, the Duke of York sent the following reply to the Lord Mayor: "Please accept and convey to the citizens of London our sincere thanks for their kind congratulations, which we deeply appreciate. The Duchess and baby are making excellent progress.- ALBERT."

The Times, April 22, 1926

The Duke and Duchess of York with their daughter, Princess Elizabeth.

A ROYAL CHILDHOOD
by Kate Williams

On December 10, 1936, the ten-year old Princess Elizabeth of York was at home at No. 145 Piccadilly with her sister, Margaret. Preparing to write up her notes from her swimming lesson, she heard shouts of "God save the King" from outside. She realised that people were calling for her father. She asked a footman the reason for the noise. He told her – and she dashed straight up the stairs to Margaret. "Uncle David is going away and isn't coming back, and Papa is going to be King."

"Does that mean you will have to be the next Queen?" demanded Margaret, only six.

"Yes, some day," said her sister. "Poor you," replied Margaret.

Elizabeth was unruffled. As she would do throughout her life at moments of crisis, she maintained her routine. According to the diary of her governess, Marion Crawford, she sat down and began to write up her notes from the swimming lesson. She wrote at the top of the paper: Abdication Day.

Elizabeth Alexandra Mary was born in the early hours of April 21, 1926, at 17 Bruton Street in Mayfair, the home of her mother's family. She was immediately everybody's favourite. "We have long wanted a child to make our happiness complete," wrote her father, Albert, or "Bertie", Duke of York. The King and Queen, stiff and even unforgiving with their own children, were delighted by their "little darling", who was third in line to the throne at birth. She was named after her mother, great-grandmother and grandmother-consorts rather than queens regnant.

"He says nothing about Victoria," George V reported of his son. "I hardly think it necessary." In other words, the princess didn't need the name of the great female monarch because she would never be Queen.

Although never intended to reign, little "Lilibet" was catapulted into the full glare of media attention. One newspaper dubbed her "the world's best-known baby". "It almost frightens me that the people love her so much," said her mother, the Duchess of York. "I hope she will be worthy of it." However, the princess was most cherished by the king. She called him "Grandpa England".

When Margaret was born, in Scotland in August 1930, Elizabeth was thrilled. "I have got a new baby sister," she told an estate tenant. "She is so very lovely." The Yorks were now "we four" or "us four", surprisingly close for the standards of the time, giggling together at bedtime in their new Piccadilly home. The property was huge by modern standards – with a lift and a ballroom – but it was a house, rather than a palace. Elizabeth and Margaret played in the gardens with the daughters of the neighbours – businessmen and doctors, rather than royals. The two sisters were cared for by the nannies Clara Knight and Margaret (or "Bobo") Macdonald, who kept them to a strict routine of meals, naps and airings.

The sisters played very different roles in the family. Elizabeth was conscientious, striving, dutiful – and so orderly that she couldn't sleep if her shoes were not parallel under her bed. Margaret was spirited and naughty – as she grew older, she blamed every fault on her invented "Cousin Halifax". The duke remarked on Elizabeth's perfectionism and indulged Margaret's silly games.

The duchess wanted her daughters to have "a really happy childhood ... and later, happy marriages". She was not a believer in too much education. The duke had been bullied at school and agreed to a light timetable. All King George wished for was that they develop a "decent hand" – because, he said, "none of my children could write properly".

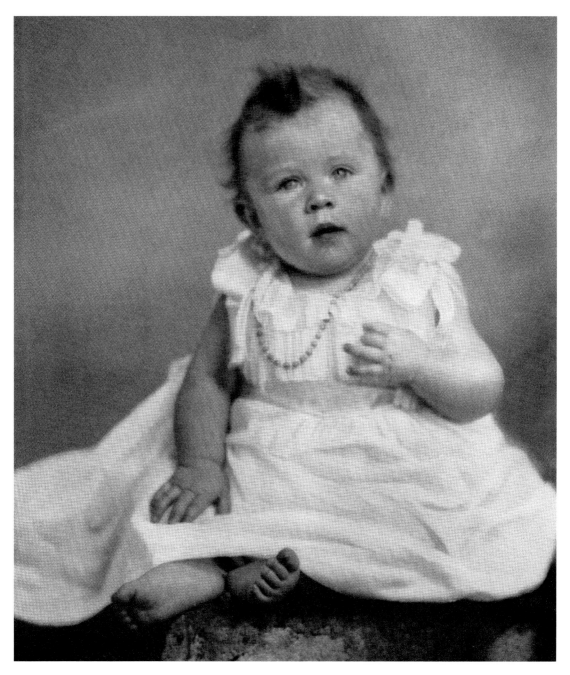

One newspaper referred to Princess Elizabeth as "the world's best-known baby".

Princess Elizabeth and Princess Margaret in 1932. The future Queen had about thirty toy horses.

Crawford came from Edinburgh to be the princesses' governess in 1933. She arrived to find the seven-year-old Elizabeth in bed, pretending to drive her horses, tying her dressing gown cords to the bedsteads. "I mostly go once or twice round the park before I sleep, you know," she said. Horse mad, the little girl had thirty or so toy horses. Every night they were fed and watered and lined up neatly outside the nursery. The girls began their day bouncing on their parents' bed. Elizabeth had lessons from 9.30am until 11am with Crawford. The rest of the day was passed in exercise, dancing, singing, a short rest and an hour in which "Crawfie" read to her. The princesses played with their mother before supper and enjoyed card games before bed. Queen Mary thought Elizabeth needed more history, but the Yorks preferred their daughters to be running about outside.

In 1936 everything changed. "It was plain to everyone that there was a sudden shadow over the house," Crawford wrote. Elizabeth's grandfather died within a year of his Silver Jubilee. At the end of the year Edward, Prince of Wales, abdicated to marry Wallis Simpson and Elizabeth's father, poor, unprepossessing Bertie, had to become George VI.

"I was overwhelmed," the new King said. Unlike his brother, however, he had a trump card in a perfect little family.

Elizabeth was destined now for quite a different future. She was heir to the throne. Elizabeth attended her father's coronation in 1937. She sat with Queen Mary and Margaret and took a keen interest in proceedings. "I thought it all very, very wonderful," she wrote in a little book she made for her parents.

The family had to leave their Piccadilly home for the cavernous and rather gloomy Buckingham Palace. Crawfie compared it to "camping in a museum" and Lilibet thought it so big that "people need bicycles". There were dozens of staff and police detectives on guard. The new King and Queen no longer had the time to play every day with their children, but the Queen tried to give her daughters a "normal" childhood, arranging the 1st Buckingham Palace Girl Guides pack, with an attached set of Brownies for the girls. Elizabeth and

Margaret practised semaphore in the palace corridors and cooked sausages over fires in the gardens.

Queen Mary's enthusiasm for history finally won the day. In 1938 Elizabeth was sent to Eton twice a week to learn constitutional history from the provost of the school, Henry Marten. As they ploughed through the constitutional scholarship of Sir William Anson, Marten told her that the British monarchy's strength was its adaptability, and he talked of the importance of broadcasting. As he saw it, speaking directly to the subjects via the radio encouraged their loyalty. It was a useful lesson for Elizabeth, who would go on to become an accomplished broadcaster.

The war changed everything for "us four".

The girls moved to Windsor, Elizabeth begging her father for a greater role. Her work with the Auxiliary Territorial Service (ATS) was vital to war propaganda – and throughout her life she has felt a special bond with war veterans. After the war the 19-year-old princess was flung once more into the public eye. Her days were taken up with correspondence and public engagements – opening factories, presenting prizes, addressing delegations and Girl Guides – as well as being colonel of the Grenadier Guards.

The palace did, however, turn down the offer of an honorary degree from Cambridge University. It wouldn't do for the princess to seem too intellectual.

For her 21st birthday Elizabeth received a car from her parents with the numberplate HRHL. On the day itself she was in South Africa on tour. She gave a speech on the radio to the Empire and Commonwealth. As she said: "I can make my solemn act of dedication with a whole Empire listening." Her dedication was one of self-sacrifice and duty. People all over the world listened as she said: "I declare before you all that my whole life, whether it be long or short, shall be devoted to your service."

She was ready to be Queen.

Elizabeth, shown here in 1932, took ballet lessons after her studies.

The Queen's love of horses has endured throughout her life.

King George VI and Queen Elizabeth with Princess Elizabeth and Princess Margaret in the grounds of Windsor Castle in 1936.

Princess Elizabeth with her mother and sister in 1940, the year following the outbreak of the Second World War.

The teenage princess studied constitutional history to prepare for her new destiny.

~ King Edward's Farewell ~

At 10 o'clock last night Sir John Reith announced on the wireless:–

"This is Windsor Castle. His Royal Highness Prince Edward."

The former King then broadcast the following message:–

At long last I am able to say a few words of my own. I have never wanted to withhold anything, but until now it has not been constitutionally possible for me to speak. A few hours ago I discharged my last duty as King and Emperor, and now that I have been succeeded by my brother, the Duke of York, my first words must be to declare my allegiance to him. This I do with all my heart. You all know the reasons which have impelled me to renounce the Throne. But I want you to understand that in making up my mind I did not forget the country or the Empire which as Prince of Wales, and lately as King, I have for 25 years tried to serve. But you must believe me when I tell you that I have found it impossible to carry the heavy burden of responsibility and to discharge my duties as King as I would wish to do without the help and support of the woman I love. And I want you to know that the decision I have made has been mine and mine alone. This was a thing I had to judge entirely for myself. The other person more nearly concerned has tried up to the last to persuade me to take a different course. I have made this, the most serious decision of my life, only upon the single thought of what would in the end be best for all. This decision has been made less difficult to me by the sure knowledge that my brother, with his long training in the public affairs of this country and with his fine qualities, will be able to take my place forthwith, without interruption or injury to the life and progress of the Empire.

And he has one matchless blessing, enjoyed by so many of you and not bestowed on me – a happy home with his wife and children.

The Times, December 12, 1936

As Prince of Wales, Edward VIII served in the Grenadier Guards during the First World War. He became King when his father, George V, died in 1936, but he abdicated in order to marry Wallis Simpson, an American divorcee.

A PRINCESS AT WAR

by Valentine Low

On the evening of September 3, 1939, King George VI broadcast to the nation: "For the second time in the lives of most of us, we are at war." Princess Elizabeth and Princess Margaret sat close to the wireless in Scotland, listening. Elizabeth was 13.

The princesses remained in Scotland until after Christmas, when they moved to Royal Lodge, then Windsor Castle. The King and Queen lived at Buckingham Palace and refused to listen to government pleas that they should escape to Canada or the United States. As the Queen said: "The children will not leave unless I do. I shall not leave until their father does, and the King will not leave the country under any circumstances whatsoever." In Windsor the children continued lessons, ate their rations in darkness and spent evenings in the air-raid shelter under the castle. They were ready to flee at any time and slept in "siren suits": all-in-ones beloved of Winston Churchill.

Prewar, suggestions that Elizabeth might broadcast on the radio were rebuffed. In 1940, the palace changed its mind. Elizabeth gave a speech during Children's Hour on the BBC to Britain and North America, aimed at evacuees. As she told them, she and Margaret "feel so much for you, as we know from experience what it means to be away from those we love most of all". It was a propaganda hit in America.

Yet Elizabeth longed for a greater role in the war effort. The King refused. When she turned 16, Elizabeth graduated from the Girl Guides to the Sea Rangers (senior Guides had been known as Rangers since 1920). The Sea Rangers focused on naval training and Elizabeth gained her boating permit and practised dinghy sailing – and went on short camps where she had to do the washing-up. In 1945 she was promoted to Sea Ranger Commodore.

Princess Margaret looks on as Princess Elizabeth broadcasts in 1940.

The princess during ATS training, under the watchful eye of her mother, Queen Elizabeth, in 1945.

Yet Elizabeth wanted to do more. She begged her father to let her join the services. "I ought to do as other girls of my age do," she said. Finally, the King allowed her to join the Auxiliary Territorial Service (ATS) in March of the same year. By this point women had adopted nearly all army driving work.

Elizabeth didn't sleep in the camp dorm in Aldershot. She returned to Windsor each night. However, she worked hard. She had never even held a spanner before, and so, as she said, "everything I learnt was brand new to me – all the oddities of the inside of the car and all the intricacies of map-reading". She later told the politician Barbara Castle that it had been the only time she had been able to test herself against people the same age as her. Photographs of her at work appeared on the cover of *Time* magazine and every Allied newspaper. She loved her work, and found driving thrilling.

On May 7, 1945, the BBC interrupted a piano recital to announce that the next day would be known as Victory in Europe day. On May 8, the princesses appeared on the balcony of Buckingham Palace, Elizabeth wearing her ATS uniform. That night she and Margaret, with their governesses and some guards, set off to celebrate, dashing incognito through the crowds. As Elizabeth remembered, "all of us were swept along by tides of happiness and relief".

Princess Elizabeth takes the wheel of an ATS ambulance in 1945.

Princess Elizabeth, Preparation for Future Responsibilities

Princess Elizabeth will be 18 years old next Friday. Notwithstanding a recent Act, correcting a constitutional anomaly, which has drawn special attention to the birthday, this is neither a coming-of-age nor a "coming out." But 18 is something of a landmark in any girl's life, whether she be princess or milkmaid; and especially in wartime, for it is the age of registration. Princess Elizabeth is no longer a child; she is already beginning to move more freely among her future subjects. Without any "building up" of an entrance, a new character has slipped demurely upon the stage of public life. She has few lines to speak at present, but in a later act she will have many. The audience will watch with a lively curiosity the gradual revelation of her character. She is, of course, like any young girl, very much the product of her upbringing. The lines, though clear, are lightly traced. It is for life to determine which of them shall be more deeply etched.

It has been the first care of their Majesties to secure to their daughters a natural and normal childhood; to prepare the heiress indeed for her future responsibilities, but to shield her from their premature impact. They have aimed at providing the sort of environment that the most enlightened English parents of their own generation would best like their children to grow up in: a comfortable and cultivated home, with an atmosphere of affection, easy manners, and reasonable discipline.

The real director of the Princess's education has been and is the Queen, its immediate supervisor a young Edinburgh graduate, Miss Crawford, who has upheld through the years of tutelage the standards of simple living and honest thinking that Scotland peculiarly respects. Specialist teachers have been called in to help; but the Princess has not been encouraged, nor has she desired, to become a specialist.

A sound physical education has provided the background of all her studies. She is a good horsewoman, and rather more than a good swimmer, and she enjoys all the outdoor sports and amusements natural to her age. War, which in some ways has been cramping for her, has in this respect been kind. She has had to share the common lot of her contemporaries in frequent separation from her parents; on the other hand, she has enjoyed a greater proportion of country life than might have fallen to her in peace. On the academic side the Princess's education has been mostly in modern subjects, and pursued on a wide front. Like some others of her sex, she is no mathematician. But she took kindly to modern languages, and speaks both French and German fluently and well. She has read many of the classics of French literature, and of course many more of English. If her literary education shows any bias it is towards history, as is proper to one called to her peculiar destiny…

Princess Elizabeth stands for the generation that will inherit the coming victory – she will live in a new world, and will be the representative of those who have to mould it. None may prophesy what the circumstances of their and her future will be; what is essential above all is the ability to master them, however unexpected the form they take. Freshness, simplicity, and the undiminished capacity to learn – all native qualities of youth – are the condition of achieving that mastery. These have been preserved in Princess Elizabeth partly by her education, but even more by her own innate sense of their supreme value.

The Times, April 17, 1944

Princess Elizabeth (left) with her mother, Queen Elizabeth, and sister, Princess Margaret, in 1944.

Princess Elizabeth shortly after she turned 18, holding Susan the corgi.

Night Scenes in London, Royal Family on Palace Balcony, Rejoicing Crowds

The biggest crowd seen outside Buckingham Palace since the Silver Jubilee, outnumbering even those of the Coronation, greeted the King and Queen and the two Princesses when they appeared on the balcony last night. The people packed the pavements and the roadway in front of the Palace, and for a long way down The Mall. They stood in silence listening to the King's broadcast speech, and at the end of it raised a great cheer, and sang the National Anthem. Then the crowd began to chant: "We want the King." A few minutes later the King and Queen appeared on the balcony with the Princesses, and waved and smiled to the crowds. The King was in naval uniform, and the Queen was wearing a white ermine wrap over her evening gown and had a diamond tiara in her hair. For five minutes there was a tumult of cheering.

About 10.45 the King and Queen and the Princesses again came out on to the balcony, where they stayed about 10 minutes, waving to the crowd in response to cheers. Shortly before midnight, when searchlights were being flashed across the sky, their Majesties appeared on the balcony again, and remained there for a few minutes. When they returned to the palace most of the crowd left for home. Earlier the two Princesses, escorted by Guards officers, had left the palace to mingle with the crowd outside.

Everywhere crowds listened silently to the loud-speaker relays of the King's speech. Some 60,000 people in Trafalgar Square, bareheaded, joined in singing the National Anthem. A crowd of about 10,000 listened in Parliament Square. In Whitehall, as soon as the King had finished speaking, bandsmen of the Grenadier Guards played outside the Ministry of Health and the crowd sang and danced. There was also dancing in other parts of London.

Floodlighting drew great crowds to Buckingham Palace after dark. St. Paul's Cathedral was also impressively floodlit, by A.T.S. girls. Trafalgar Square was flooded with light as Nelson's Column was illuminated, and the crowd grew to about 100,000 as streams of people converged on the square.

The Times, May 9, 1945

Crowds gather to see the royal family waving from the balcony of Buckingham Palace on VE Day.

Princess Elizabeth, with Queen Elizabeth, King George VI and Princess Margaret on the balcony of Buckingham Palace on VE Day, May 8, 1945.

A PRINCESS
IN LOVE

"HOW HIGH HE CAN JUMP!"

by Kate Williams

"How high he can jump!" said Elizabeth to Marion Crawford, in July 1939. The princess and her governess were watching the handsome 18-year-old cadet Prince Philip of Greece leaping over nets on the tennis courts, while her parents made an official visit to the Royal Naval College in Dartmouth. It was 1939, just before the outbreak of the war. Elizabeth was 13 and had lived a sheltered life. Her second cousin once removed, clever, international Philip of Greece was a revelation.

Elizabeth was entranced, much to the delight of Philip's uncle Dickie Mountbatten, who had engineered the meeting. Philip was invited to join the family for tea on the royal yacht, moored near by – and Elizabeth watched, fascinated, as Philip ate a banana split. When the royal yacht departed Dartmouth, the cadets followed in their little boats, until the King commanded them to turn back. They obeyed – apart from Prince Philip, who rowed hard after them. Elizabeth watched him through her binoculars. Officials shouted at Philip through a megaphone until he finally turned – but the die had been cast. Philip found the young princess very appealing – cheerful and practical, she was unlike his fragile mother.

Philip was born in Corfu in 1921, the only son, and fifth and final child, of Prince Andrew of Greece and Denmark and Princess Alice of Battenberg. When Philip was one, a popular uprising forced his uncle King Constantine I of Greece to abdicate, and Prince Andrew was exiled from Greece. The family set up in Paris but disintegrated – his mother was put in an asylum and his father took a mistress. Philip was sent to boarding schools and flourished at Gordonstoun in Scotland before going to Dartmouth.

Princess Elizabeth (front, third from left), with King George VI, Lord Louis Mountbatten, known as Dickie to the family, (standing, third from right) and Queen Elizabeth (centre front) during the visit to the Royal Naval College, Dartmouth, 1939. It is thought that this is where Princess Elizabeth first met Prince Philip (standing, second from right).

Prince Philip was born in Corfu, Greece, in 1921. He is pictured here in his naval uniform.

Elizabeth and Philip attend the wedding of Lady Patricia Mountbatten,
Philip's first cousin, in 1946 – the year before they became engaged.

During the war, Philip wrote regularly to Elizabeth and came to stay for Christmas in 1943. With the end of hostilities, he came to court the 19-year-old future queen in earnest. Occasionally they went to concerts or restaurants; at other times they stayed in the nursery with Margaret and drank orangeade. Elizabeth's circle was not enthusiastic. The King and Queen wished her to "see more of the world" and "meet more men" before marrying. There was concern among courtiers that Philip was not quite the right sort – "no gentleman" – and he signed visitors' books as of "no fixed abode". Elizabeth refused to listen. She had been set on Philip since Dartmouth; the separation of war had only intensified the romance. The King had to relent. The engagement was announced on July 9, 1947, with the wedding fixed for November 20.

The government and courtiers worried that a lavish ceremony might infuriate a population deep in a postwar recession. However, Winston Churchill called it "a flash of colour on the hard road we have to travel" – and his view won. The marriage of the young princess and her handsome prince would be as magnificent as possible. Yet the day could not be a bank holiday; one day off might plunge the faltering economy into dire straits. Clothes rationing was still in force and thousands of women donated clothing coupons for the dress – but the palace returned them, because coupons could not be transferred. The Privy Purse found the money for the silk and Norman Hartnell designed the dress, inspired by Botticelli's *Primavera*.

Three thousand presents poured in from all over the world – and half were put on display. Elizabeth received jewels, china, vases, a racehorse, a home cinema, more than 150 pairs of silk stockings, and 500 cans of tinned pineapple from the governor of Queensland. Perhaps the oddest was two pieces of toast, sent by two young women in London who had burnt it in excitement when they heard about the engagement on the wireless.

Princess Elizabeth and Prince Philip at Buckingham Palace on July 10, 1947, after their engagement was announced.

Two nights before the wedding, the King and Queen held a ball for the royal guests at Buckingham Palace. The King led a conga through the royal apartments. It was a true postwar jamboree. Among those not invited, however, were Philip's three surviving sisters, who were married to German princes. Also staying at home were the Duke and Duchess of Windsor. Neither the princess nor her mother could forgive him for abdicating.

"I can't believe it's really happening," Elizabeth said to her old governess on the morning. At Westminster Abbey, the King escorted his daughter up the aisle, followed by her two five-year-old pageboys, cousins Prince Michael of Kent and Prince William of Gloucester, Princess Margaret and seven other bridesmaids. About 2,000 people were crammed into the stalls – the choir had to sit in the organ loft with the radio commentators. Elizabeth made her vows and promised to obey her husband – which would be technically impossible when she became Queen.

After the ceremony, 150 guests travelled to Buckingham Palace to dine on partridge casserole (partridges were unrationed) and Bombe Glacée Princess Elizabeth. The cake was created by supplies sent by the Australian Girl Guides, and stood 9ft high and weighed 500lb. While guests dined, news footage was packed up and sent all over the world.

The couple left for their honeymoon first to Hampshire, then Birkhall on the Balmoral estate, through cheering crowds, despite the rain. At the palace, the royal family felt rather deflated. "I can't imagine life without her," said Margaret. Elizabeth had enjoyed the most wonderful day. "I was so happy and enjoying myself so much that I became completely selfish," she wrote to her mother. She hoped that from now on the government would see her as an adult rather than a child.

The newly married couple walk down the aisle of Westminster Abbey.

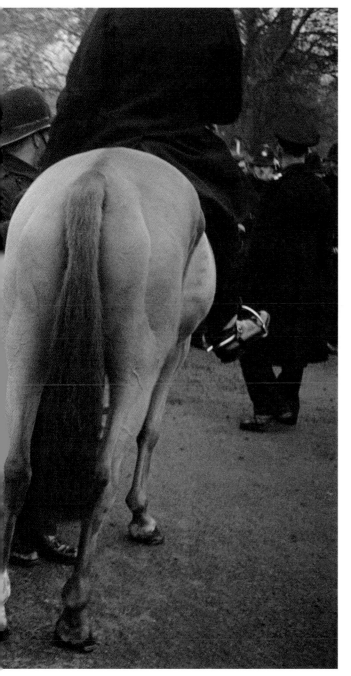

*Police hold back
crowds outside
Buckingham Palace
after the wedding.*

Marriage of Princess Elizabeth.
The Ceremony in the Abbey.

By a spontaneous gesture the whole company in the nave rose in their places to honour the entry of Mr. Churchill as he walked alone to his stall in the choir. At 11 o'clock the Precentor and two Minor Canons, vested in copes of stately gold and crimson, escorted to their places in the sanctuary the first procession of royal guests, including Lord and Lady Mountbatten and other near relatives of the bridegroom. A tumult of cheering outside the Abbey at 11.16 distracted the attention of the congregation from the arrival of the Duke of Edinburgh and his groomsman, Lord Milford Haven, who slipped in by way of Poets' Corner in the inconspicuous manner of the bridegroom's party at any ordinary wedding. This great ovation saluted the arrival of the Queen's procession, which now, meeting Queen Mary at the west door, moved with measured pace up the whole length of nave and sacrarium and were conducted to chairs within the sanctuary. The mothers of bride and bridegroom walked together, until Princess Andrew left the Queen to go to the gospel side, with the bridegroom's other relatives; Queen Mary followed with the King of Norway. When the bride's family had taken their places the front row was occupied by the Queen, Queen Mary, both of these wearing the ribbon of the Garter, the Duke of Gloucester, in khaki, and the Duchess, the King of Norway, the Duchess of Kent, and the young Duke in a kilt of Royal Stuart tartan. Next to arrive was the procession of the visiting clergy, the two archbishops, with white and gold mitres and the crosses of Canterbury and York carried before them, and with them the Moderator of the General Assembly of the Church of Scotland. The prelates went to the sedilia on the south side of the altar. Meanwhile the collegium of the Abbey itself, not only the Dean and Chapter but the lay vicars, the choristers, and the King's scholars – that privileged body who represent the voice of the lieges in the acclamation of the crowned King – had gone down in procession to the west door to meet the bride. A fanfare of silver trumpets, sounded in King Henry V's chantry above the shrine, went pealing up to the ancient vault; and precisely at half past 11 the entire college bowed to their Sovereign and Visitor as he entered the Abbey Church with the bride upon his arm. According to the custom of royal brides the Princess wore her veil so that her face was not covered, and she looked at once happy and singularly childlike as she followed the great procession of clergy up the nave, directing a shy smile towards a group of former members of the Royal Household who were sitting on the right. But the expression in the eyes of the King was that of any father who is filled at once with pride in the daughter he is handing into another's care and with unfeigned delight in the happiness she has found. The clergy parted to left and right as they reached their stalls, and the bridegroom and groomsman emerged from their inconspicuous place to form a row of four with the King and the Princess at the top of the sanctuary steps. Behind the bride her two pages, Prince William of Gloucester and Prince Michael of Kent, in white shirts and tartan kilts, held her train clear of the lowest step, and behind them again the eight bridesmaids, all in white with white wreaths and bouquets, stood in the gangway under the lantern, in the middle of the space that at a coronation is called the theatre. As the procession advanced the choir had been singing the hymn "Praise, my soul, the King of Heaven"; with its last notes Princess Margaret stepped forward to take the flowers from her sister's hands, and the Dean, bowing to the King, began the marriage service.

For the signing of the register the bride and bridegroom passed behind the altar into the Confessor's Shrine, and the King and Queen, Princess Andrew, Princess Margaret, the Duke of Gloucester, the King of Norway, and Lord Milford Haven accompanied them. In their absence the choir sang that anthem of Samuel Wesley which sounds with such notes of victory, confidence and praise its many variations on the phrase "the word of the Lord endureth for ever". It ended, and the Kneller Hall trumpets pealed forth again from King Henry's Chantry, in a fanfare that seemed yet prouder and richer than that which had greeted the entrance of the bride. The banners of the Abbey were brought out into the sanctuary facing the doors of the shrine, whence the royal family emerged, led by the Queen, and returned to their places. Last of all came the bride and bridegroom, walking hand in hand, the bride's train carried for the moment by Princess Margaret. As they passed down the line they paused opposite to Queen Mary, and made reverence with curtsy and a deep bow. It was a charming epilogue to a ceremony full of beautiful associations; and then, still walking hand in hand, with joy in their eyes and pride and hope in their mien, they passed down through choir and nave and went out to meet the plaudits of the people.

The Times, November 21, 1947

Princess Elizabeth and Prince Philip wave to the crowds from the balcony of Buckingham Palace on their wedding day.

The royal wedding, November 20, 1947: Princess Elizabeth's coach and escort.

The princess and her new husband leave Westminster Abbey after their wedding cerermony.

The married couple.

HIS OWN MAN
by The Times & James Owen

Whatever the subsequent frustrations caused him by his role as Elizabeth's husband – and there were many – Philip would always remain true to himself. Indeed, it was this independence of mind, this certainty of self, this tireless masculinity, that had attracted her to him. These qualities also enabled him, more than was perhaps appreciated during his lifetime, to become the most successful of consorts.

Philip's character was forged during an upbringing that obliged him to become self-reliant at an unusually early age. A great-great-grandson of Queen Victoria, he was born into the house of Schleswig-Holstein-Sonderburg-Glücksburg, Danish aristocrats who had been placed on the Greek throne in 1863.

In 1922, a year after Philip's birth, a revolution stemming from Greece's defeats in Turkey led to the abdication of his uncle the King (whose own father had been assassinated in 1913). Soon after, the royal family was forced into exile, although the monarchy would be restored in 1935.

By then, however, Philip was following his own destiny. His parents had moved to Paris, but before Philip was ten his father, Prince Andrew, a soldier who had been blamed for Greece's military failings, had become estranged from his wife, Alice. In 1930 she was hospitalised for treatment of what was diagnosed as paranoid schizophrenia.

To shield him, Philip was sent to Britain, where he was looked after by his Mountbatten cousins, whose surname he adopted. After attending Cheam, a preparatory school in Surrey, he was educated at two rather unorthodox schools. The first, Schloss Salem near the Bavarian Alps, was an institution where liberality of mind was imparted in a rugged and austere physical environment.

Prince Philip (centre) was born into the Greek royal family, but spent most of his life as a pillar of the British royal family, as the Duke of Edinburgh.

When the Nazis forced the school's Jewish founder, Kurt Hahn, to flee, he established a new school in a new country: Gordonstoun, near Inverness in Scotland. Philip followed, and thrived. Hahn's early appraisals of his pupil – "lively intelligence", "meticulous attention to detail and pride of workmanship", "capacity to derive great fun from small incidents" – continued to ring true. Unlike many of his class, Philip was also open-minded and curious about the world.

In 1939, at the age of 18, Philip entered the Royal Naval College at Dartmouth in Devon. He graduated top of his class, having received commendations including Best Cadet. His capability was apparent from the start and, had his life gone differently, he would undoubtedly have risen to the top of the service on his own merits.

During the war, Philip served on battleships and saw combat in different parts of the world. In the Mediterranean he was involved in the battle for Crete and saw action against the Italian fleet at Cape Matapan, where he was mentioned in despatches for his conduct. In 1945 he witnessed the Japanese surrender at Tokyo Bay.

The man that Elizabeth decided to marry had much more experience of the world than she. Despite this, Philip knew that as a consort he would have to "fit into the institution" and avoid "getting at cross-purposes, usurping others' authority".

Even so, the progressive naval officer was determined to dispense with much of the flummery at court. When he and the Queen moved into Buckingham Palace, he noticed that a bottle of whisky was placed by the Queen's bed each night. It transpired that this had been a request of Queen Victoria's which had never been changed. Philip rescinded the request. He also had dishwashers installed in the kitchens and put an end to the 18th-century practice of footmen wearing powdered wigs.

Prince Philip talks with his uncle, Lord Mountbatten, in 1948.

Philip's urge for change would often be thwarted by the conservatism of courtiers. Clashes were inevitable, not least with the Queen Mother, who at first refused to move out of Buckingham Palace, and these were aggravated by the duke's forthright, sometimes abrupt manner – the cause of the gaffes with which Philip later became associated in the public mind.

From the start Philip showed a fierce resolution to protect his wife from the increasing intrusion of the press and palace diary-managers. The greater the nuisance, the more his irritation would show. Nor did he ever have much time for politicians.

He retained his interest in science, engineering and technology – of which he would become a champion in the Fifties – as well as, perhaps more surprisingly, an interest in modern art. His most enduring achievement, however, conceived as early as 1956, was the Duke of Edinburgh's Award, and young people remained one of the prince's abiding concerns.

Philip's father had died in Monte Carlo in 1944, having not seen his son (or wife) for five years. As a father himself, Philip would come to expect a great deal of his children, and would sometimes be disappointed. Famously, he resented not being able to give his children his own (adopted) surname, claiming that he had so little input in such decisions that he was nothing more than an "amoeba". Moreover, his relationship with his eldest son, Charles, would not be easy – the two men had very different personalities.

In many ways, the duke and the Queen also led separate lives. They had their own dining rooms, sitting rooms and bathrooms, and the intimate side of Philip's life inevitably became a matter for speculation. His continued attraction to beautiful women after his marriage was certainly no secret, but his bond with his wife rested on deeper foundations.

Humour was a bedrock of their relationship, for he could always make her giggle. Reunited with the Queen at the end of her coronation, her husband eyed her crown and remarked: "Where did you get that hat?"

Prince Philip with his son, Prince Charles, in 1952. Philip and Charles later had a rather difficult relationship.

STRENGTH AND STAY

by Sally Bedell Smith

The indelible image of the Diamond Jubilee weekend in June 2012 was of the Queen and the Duke of Edinburgh standing on the upper deck of the royal barge for nearly four hours in the rain. Aged 86 and 90, enduring chill and blustery winds, they showed fortitude as well as gratitude to the 1.2 million people along the banks of the Thames.

It was everything that symbolised the royal couple. They were tough, stoic, duty-bound, a team. A beacon of continuity throughout decades of change, they set an example and solidified the traditions that help to bind the nation.

Their mutual devotion radiated a "sense of unqualified commitment that has been so characteristic of every aspect of this reign", said the Archbishop of Canterbury Rowan Williams when they celebrated their 60th wedding anniversary in 2007. Among the places they visited that year was Malta, where they had enjoyed a carefree existence as a young married couple when Philip was posted with the Royal Navy.

In 2015 they returned to the island nation for a state visit – a sentimental three days that took them back to favourite haunts such as the Marsa racecourse, where Princess Elizabeth had watched her husband play polo. On the first night they attended a reception for Malta's great and good. It had been a long day that included a three-hour flight and a welcoming ceremony, yet the Queen was animated and engaged as she circulated through the crowd, and Philip left a trail of laughter.

If the Queen was constant and calm, the Duke of Edinburgh was a spritz of vinegar with his irreverent and sometimes caustic comments. However, he always said "supporting the Queen" was his primary purpose as her consort and he held true to this for more than seven extraordinary decades. Her marriage to her "strength and stay" arguably held the royal family together through the divorces of three of their four children, and the harrowing week

The royal couple celebrate their silver wedding anniversary at Balmoral in 1972.

The princess and the duke pictured at Broadlands, Hampshire, in 1947, shortly after their wedding.

after the death of Diana, Princess of Wales. For Britain and the Commonwealth, their remarkable partnership created the most successful monarchy in history.

Princess Elizabeth could have chosen from what her friend Lady Glenconner called "a whole battalion of lively young men", English aristocrats with vast landholdings and wealth. Yet at the unlikely age of 13 she fell in love when she first spent an afternoon with 18-year-old Prince Philip of Greece. He was a naval officer in training and a distant cousin also descended from Queen Victoria and Prince Albert. He had very little money but he was strikingly handsome, confident, intelligent, breezy and energetic.

In the ensuing years Princess Elizabeth came to view Philip as a man of ideas and appealing complexity who would be neither easy nor boring but would share her commitment to duty and service. Despite a protective shell formed during a rootless childhood when he was neglected for long periods by his divorced parents, "Philip had a capacity for love which was waiting to be unlocked", said their mutual cousin Patricia Mountbatten.

Elizabeth "would not have been a difficult person to love", she added. "She was beautiful, amusing and gay. She was fun to take dancing or to the theatre." Her curly brown hair framed her porcelain complexion, with cheeks that the photographer Cecil Beaton described as "sugar-pink", vivid blue eyes, an ample mouth that widened into a dazzling smile, and an infectious laugh.

They were married on November 20, 1947, and spent their honeymoon at Birkhall, the 18th-century lodge on the Balmoral estate. "Philip is an angel," Princess Elizabeth wrote to her mother, "he is so kind and thoughtful." He in turn wrote to his mother-in-law: "My ambition is to weld the two of us into a new combined existence that will not only be able to withstand the shocks directed at us but will also have a positive existence for the good."

To a remarkable degree, that wish came true. They had only a few years together before she assumed the burdens of the crown at the tender age of 25. Their time in Malta from 1949 to 1951 was the closest Princess Elizabeth came to an ordinary existence – socialising with other officers' wives, going to the hair salon, even carrying her own cash, although shopkeepers noted "she was slow in handling money".

It was Philip who broke the news to his wife in 1952 that her father had died at the age of 56 and that she was now the Queen. In the beginning Philip was viewed with suspicion by the old-style courtiers surrounding his wife. He was excluded from the substance of the Queen's official life, with no access to the state papers in her daily boxes. Yet he carved out a significant role for himself as a patron of more than 800 charities and advocate for causes from wildlife conservation to youth fitness, even as his wife came to rely on him for advice when making tough decisions.

If her advisers brought a question to her on a matter outside her head-of-state role, she asked them first to find out what Philip thought. Her approach to problems is to look at the big picture and ask for other options, while Philip drilled down and got to the heart of a problem – what one of her advisers called "a defence staff rigour", with an ability to "pull an idea to bits, find the good parts and the parts that need work". Her advisers knew that if her husband was happy with an idea, she probably would be as well. Early on, Philip saw the potential of television for the monarchy. He encouraged the Queen to use it and even tutored her on how to read from an Autocue for her first televised speech in 1957.

On their trips around the United Kingdom and overseas, they perfected a choreography of turns and cues that appeared effortless. He would watch her intently during their walkabouts to see whether she needed any assistance. He would often spot people who couldn't see her – children in particular – and guide them out of the crowd to a better vantage point. When the Queen needed a boost, he was there with a humorous aside: "Don't look so sad, sausage."

The Queen gets the giggles as she passes the Duke of Edinburgh in uniform at Buckingham Palace in 2005.

In the Solomon Islands in 1982, during their South Pacific tour.

*One of a series of portraits taken at Buckingham Palace in November 2001
to commemorate the Golden Jubilee the next year.*

On board a private jet – a scene from the 1969 BBC film Royal Family.

In a greenhouse at Balmoral, 1972.

*Arriving at St Paul's Cathedral for a service of thanksgiving held in honour
of the Queen's 80th birthday, June 15, 2006.*

I VOW TO THEE,
MY COUNTRY

LONG LIVE THE QUEEN
by Valentine Low

Because King George VI died in his sleep, of a coronary thrombosis, it is hard to put an exact time on the moment Princess Elizabeth became Queen. This much is certain, however: she was high up in a fig tree in Kenya, surrounded by wild animals, and did not hear the news until some hours later.

She and Philip were staying at Treetops, a game-viewing lodge in a tree overlooking a waterhole where they could watch the wildlife, on the first leg of a tour that was due to take them to Australia and New Zealand.

On the morning of February 6, 1952, knowing nothing of what had happened at home, they returned to Sagana Lodge, the farm given to them by the Kenyan government as a wedding present. Eventually Michael Parker, one of the royal party, was told the news over the phone by Martin Charteris, the Queen's private secretary, who was at a hotel a few miles away.

Parker crept around the house to attract Philip's attention and beckoned him out on to the lawn. The news left the prince utterly shocked. "He looked," Parker recalled, "as if you'd dropped half the world on him."

By the time Charteris found the new Queen, she was at her desk drafting letters of apology for the cancellation of the tour. "What are you going to call yourself?" he asked. "My own name, of course," she replied. "What else?"

On her way back to London she changed from the jeans she had been wearing at Sagana Lodge into the mourning clothes that always travelled with her. Outwardly she was calm, a woman who despite her relative youth – she was 25 – appeared ready for the role that fate had thrust upon her; inside, she was doing her best to conceal the grief she felt at the loss of her father.

On the tarmac at Heathrow, after a 24-hour journey, she was met by Winston Churchill. The prime minister – who was accompanied by the leader of the opposition Clement Attlee; the lord president of the council

Lord Wootton; and the foreign secretary Anthony Eden – seemed so overcome by emotion that he could not speak.

The next day, at St James's Palace, at her formal proclamation as Queen, Elizabeth spoke of "this heavy task that has been laid upon me so early in my life". She said: "My heart is too full for me to say more to you today than that I shall always work, as my father did throughout his reign, to uphold constitutional government and to advance the happiness and prosperity of my peoples, spread as they are all the world over."

It is a promise she has kept for longer, and with a greater devotion to duty, than anyone might have imagined.

Upon hearing the news of the death of her father, the new Queen appeared outwardly calm.

~ Death of the King ~

It is with profound regret that we announce the death of the King at Sandringham early yesterday. The following statement was issued from Buckingham Palace. "It was announced from Sandringham at 10.45 a.m. today, February 6, 1952, that the King, who retired to rest last night in his usual health, passed peacefully away in his sleep early this morning." The Duke of Edinburgh broke the news to the new Queen in Kenya. After hurried preparations had been made, they flew from the little landing ground near Nyeri to Entebbe, Uganda, to join their airliner Atalanta. A tropical storm delayed their departure from Entebbe for two hours. They left just before midnight (8.47 p.m. G.M.T.) and are expected to reach London at 4.30 p.m. today. The Queen and Princess Margaret were at Sandringham when the King died. His Majesty had been out shooting on the previous day. The Accession Council, at a brief meeting at 5 p.m. yesterday, signed the Proclamation of Queen Elizabeth II.

This is described in the constitutional textbooks as a body which is something more than the Privy Council and one which represents "a more ancient assemblage, the Witan or Commune Concilium meeting to choose and proclaim" the new Sovereign. The large attendance at the Council included the Lord President, Lord Woolton, the Prime Minister, the Foreign Secretary, the Chancellor of the Exchequer, Mr. Attlee, Mr. Herbert Morrison, many other Ministers, Opposition front benchers and private members of Parliament who are Privy Councillors, Lord Mountbatten, representatives of several other countries of the Commonwealth, and the Lord Mayor and other representatives of the City of London. One of the Commonwealth Privy Councillors at St. James's Palace was Sir Arthur Fadden, Deputy Prime Minister of Australia. He heard of the King's death and the Council meeting while he was visiting Napoleon's tomb in Paris. He chartered a special aeroplane to London and arrived at the Palace just as the Council was dispersing. He was in time to add his name to the list of signatures on the Proclamation. An interesting feature of the text of the Proclamation is the designation of Queen Elizabeth as "Head of the Commonwealth". She is the first Sovereign who has been so proclaimed on accession to the Throne.

The news of her father's death was broken to the Queen by the Duke of Edinburgh at 2.45 p.m. local time (11.45 a.m. Greenwich time). It was first given to the Royal Lodge by a representative of the East African Standard, who was reporting the royal tour and received a news agency message from his office in Nairobi, and by Major Charteris, who both spoke from the same telephone box in the Outspan Hotel, Nyeri, 17 miles from the Royal Lodge, at 2.10 p.m. Lieutenant-Commander Parker informed the Duke, and they waited until official confirmation had been received at the Royal Lodge by radio-telephone. The Duke then broke the news to his wife. She was resting after spending the night at the Treetops Hotel, in Aberdare Forest, watching big game. Arrangements for their departure were hurriedly made and the royal couple left the Lodge at 5.30 and drove to the airfield at Nanyuki, which lies on the equator.

The Queen wore a beige dress, a white hat, and white shoes, and the Duke a grey lounge suit with a black tie. The streets of Nanyuki through which they passed were filled with silent crowds. The natives said *Shauri mbaya kabisa* – "the very worst has happened" – when they heard the news. It was nearly dark when the royal car reached Nanyuki, and flares had been placed round the edge of the airfield in case they should be needed, but it was desired to avoid lighting them if possible as the grass was so dry that fire was feared. The Queen looked as if under strain when she stepped from the car, but she acted with great courage and smiled graciously at everyone.

The Times, February 7, 1952

Princess Elizabeth and the Duke of York with their corgis in July 1936,
just a few months before the duke became King.

The new Queen is met at Heathrow on February 7, 1952, by (right to left) Winston Churchill, Clement Attlee, Anthony Eden and Lord Woolton.

THE LIGHT SHINES IN THE DARKNESS

by Ian Bradley

Although reserved about what she rightly regards as a personal matter, the Queen has made no secret of her Christian faith. Together with her belief that she was called and anointed by God, it has sustained and strengthened her throughout her reign. There are very few Sundays when she is not in church, and her regular attendance is a matter of conviction rather than duty.

She was, of course, brought up in the Christian faith and schooled in the Victorian virtues of duty, discretion and dignity by her parents. There is some evidence that as a girl she felt that she was at the receiving end of rather too much religious teaching. At the age of ten she is said to have responded when asked by the Archbishop of Canterbury, Cosmo Gordon Lang, whether she would like to join him in a walk through the Sandringham gardens: "Yes, very much, but please don't tell me anything more about God. I know all about Him already."

The next year she wrote an account of her father's Coronation complaining that "at the end the service got rather boring as it was all prayers". These early protestations aside, Princess Elizabeth soon showed that she had the same strong faith as her father, grandfather and great-great- grandmother. In her first broadcast, made at the age of 14 during the darkest days of the war in October 1940, she spoke directly to children who had been evacuated from their homes, telling them: "God will care for us and give us victory and peace."

It has been in her more recent Christmas Day broadcasts that she has most clearly revealed the strength and nature of her faith. In the first five decades of her reign these were often essentially glorified travelogues. A radically new tone was introduced in the 2000 broadcast when the Queen, speaking directly to camera, made what could only be described as a personal testimony: "For me the teachings of Christ and my own personal accountability before God provide a framework in which I try to lead my life."

This particular broadcast attracted 25 times more letters to Buckingham Palace than any previous royal Christmas message.

Encouraged by its reception, the Queen has continued to make frequent allusions to her faith in subsequent Christmas broadcasts. In 2002, reflecting on a year in which she mourned the deaths of her mother and sister and celebrated her Golden Jubilee, she said: "I know just how much I rely on my own faith to guide me through the good times and the bad." In her Christmas Day broadcast in 2015, she quoted from St John's Gospel – "The light shines in the darkness, and the darkness has not overcome it" – and spoke of her personal identification with this message.

Although rooted in Protestant Christianity, and feeling most at home with its tenets and style of worship, she has reached out warmly and generously to those of other denominations and religious traditions. In her 2004 Christmas broadcast she movingly retold the parable of the Good Samaritan and called for greater understanding and respect between those of different faiths and cultures. This has been a heartfelt and oft-repeated plea, springing from her belief in the power of religion as a force for good and reconciliation, and in the continuing validity of the teachings of the world's leading faiths.

With the Archbishop of Canterbury, Rowan Williams, in 2012.

THE CORONATION
by Valentine Low

The Queen was only 25 when her father died, but for all the shock of his death she appeared to be as prepared for her new role as she ever would be. Two days later she was at St James's Palace for the Accession Council, where she made the Accession Declaration and took an oath to preserve the Church of Scotland. One of those present recalled how "a slight figure dressed in deep mourning entered the great room alone, and, with strong but perfectly controlled emotion, went through the exacting task the Constitution prescribed".

The other side of that dedication to duty has always been a tendency to traditionalism, a reluctance to change things unless there is a good reason to do so. However, that does not mean that the Queen has ever been a stick-in-the-mud, determined to adhere to the old ways at all costs. This was demonstrated early on in the volte-face made by the palace over the question of whether television cameras would be allowed into Westminster Abbey for the Coronation.

During the planning the modernisers were keen to have the ceremony televised, while the traditionalists were opposed, arguing that it was essential to preserve the mystique of royalty. It was also felt that there were moments of the ceremony that were so sacred they should remain private. The Queen sided with the traditionalists, as did Winston Churchill, who felt that allowing in television would put too much strain on the Queen, and an announcement was duly made that television cameras would be banned from the abbey.

There was immediate uproar. The papers demanded, "Let the people see the Queen", and the palace soon beat a hasty retreat. It was the Queen herself, who had originally thought that the cameras would be inappropriate, who decided it was time to listen to the people. As Sarah Bradford wrote in her biography: "When she saw how much her people wanted to see her actually crowned and how outraged they were that they should be excluded from a spectacle confined only to high officials, peers and foreigners, Elizabeth became convinced that the ban was a mistake." The television cameras were allowed into the abbey, but – in a last concession to those wanting to preserve at least some of the magic – they were not allowed to film the anointing and the communion, the most sacred parts of the service.

For everyone involved, the Coronation was heavy with the weight of symbolism. For the government, still wrestling with postwar austerity, the new Queen represented the nation's fragile hope. It was also an opportunity to promote the cause of the newly established Commonwealth, one that the Queen adopted with equal enthusiasm. When Norman Hartnell was designing her coronation dress, she asked him to embroider it with the symbols of the Commonwealth countries, such as the lotus flower of Ceylon and the wattle of Australia, as well as the traditional British emblems of the English rose, the Scottish thistle and the Welsh leek.

Above all, though, it was a solemn and sacred statement of her pledge to serve her people. After taking the Coronation Oath, in which she promised to govern her peoples – in Britain and overseas – according to their respective laws and customs, and to maintain the "Protestant reformed religion established by law", she moved to the altar and, laying a hand on the Bible, swore: "The things which I have here before promised, I will perform and keep. So help me God."

The Queen kissed the Bible and signed the oath, and then took her place in St Edward's chair, where, under a canopy held unsteadily by four Garter knights, the Archbishop of Canterbury anointed her, saying: "As Solomon was anointed by Zadok the priest and Nathan the prophet, so be thou anointed, blessed and consecrated Queen over the peoples whom the Lord thy God hath given thee to rule and govern."

*The Queen, in the Gold State Coach, passes cheering crowds
en route to Westminster Abbey for her Coronation.*

*Queen Elizabeth II and the Duke of Edinburgh wave at the crowds from the Buckingham Palace
balcony after Elizabeth's coronation on June 2, 1953.*

During Queen Elizabeth II's coronation at Westminster Abbey.

The seriousness with which the Queen regarded the promises she made that day is the key to how she has governed her life since. The fact that she regards her position not as an honour, or a privilege, or even a calling, but as a sacred duty means that she has never shrunk from her commitment to serve. On a day-to-day basis, that still can be seen in the attitude she takes to her work. She reads her red boxes without fail, from the latest cabinet minutes to the weekly summaries from her realms across the world. Whether it is the latest Foreign Office correspondence or a briefing from Canada in French (no translation required; the Queen is fluent in French), all are studied and carefully digested. She still keeps her weekly meetings with the prime minister.

"She is very assiduous and careful about reading things and when you discussed things with her, she had read them very carefully," her former deputy private secretary Mary Francis once said. "You don't very often get a question or a comment. But you know it's all sinking in and almost certainly some of it gets played back when she meets the prime minister at her weekly meeting or has her audiences with new ambassadors."

Harold Macmillan, her prime minister at the beginning of the 1960s, wrote in his diary that he was "astonished" at her grasp of detail. The Queen's dedication to duty is so much part of the fabric of the nation, an aspect of her which people have come to expect without question, that it was still taken for granted even when she reached her nineties.

Well into her ninth decade the Queen carried out a solid 400 engagements or so every year. On one notable occasion in 2014, at the end of a state visit to France that included an official ceremony in Normandy to mark the 70th anniversary of the D-Day landings, the Queen undertook a morning of engagements in Paris, only to dash back to Britain by helicopter in time for the Epsom Derby.

In 2015, the year that Elizabeth became the longest reigning monarch in British history, she undertook 341 engagements – 306 in the UK and 35 abroad. Every day she still scans newspapers and reviews her correspondence – 200 to 300 letters a day.

Whether it was conducting the state opening of parliament, hosting foreign heads of state, or laying the wreath at the Cenotaph on Remembrance Sunday, the Queen showed at 90 an energy and a resilience that would be remarkable in a woman 20 years younger.

The pandemic necessarily curtailed this programme, even as she had finally begun to entrust more of her burden to the younger generations of the royal family. Yet at not far short of 100, she remains our glorious and devoted monarch.

The newly crowned Queen on the balcony of Buckingham Palace, as Prince Charles, Princess Anne, Prince Philip, the Queen Mother and Princess Margaret look on.

The Queen Crowned at Westminster

From the moment when the great procession – as majestic as its name – made its infinitely slow progress from the west door to the Sanctuary until the last ceremonial act had been fulfilled television held it all within its compass – or nearly all. The great mystery of the Anointing was veiled from sight beneath the silken canopy and the greater solemnity of the reception of the Blessed Sacrament by the Queen and her Consort was a moment too sacred for intrusion. But millions saw the culmination of the tremendous drama when St. Edward's Crown was uplifted in a majestic gesture by the Archbishop of Canterbury and descended gently in all the flashing splendour of sovereignty on the youthful brow, bowed to receive it. The stillness and composure of that slight, graceful figure, lustrous in the stiff habiliments of monarchy, endowed the moment with an enormous sense of historic import.

The hush was soon to be engulfed in acclaim, but the effect was unforgettable. Prince Charles was there to see it, in the protective presence of his royal grandmother. A few moments later his father came to perform that humble, tender act of homage, to swear as liege man of life and limb and to salute with a kiss his Queen and his wife. It was as husband and consort, also, that he knelt beside her in one of the most moving episodes of the great ceremony to receive a special blessing from the Archbishop.

Nothing was more memorable in the long solemnities than the manner in which her Majesty bore her part in them. Not only at the Crowning but in every movement and gesture there was a deep sense of recollection. Dignity went hand in hand with modesty, simplicity with majesty, gravity with a charm which shone like crystal within all that glitter of imperial and ecclesiastical effulgence.

When the last ceremony was completed to its perfect and shapely end, and the last echo of the great Te Deum had died, when the slow recession had withdrawn its splendid tide of pomp and colour from the shining Sanctuary, the multitudes outside prepared to receive their Queen. They had shared wholeheartedly in the singing of the "Old Hundredth", which by a nice touch of imaginative forethought had joined the nation in the vocal offering of the service. And now was the moment of acclaim for their newly anointed and crowned Sovereign. To those who had borne her on her way to the Abbey with thunderous cheers were added thousands more who thronged the ribboned miles of the long return procession.

The capital had drawn to its heart a great concourse which left to a sabbath calm nearly every street outside the processional way. Rain beat heavily on the stalwarts who had braved the rigours of the waiting

hours and it was still pouring from leaden skies when the first royal processions left the Abbey. But when the state coach began to move off in the wake of the endless ranks of service men and women already in position far along the route the sun struggled through its veils. Colour leapt into splendour, and metal shone like silver.

Silvery also rang the Abbey bells, mingling with the great cheer which thundered round the Queen. Framed in the golden elaboration of the coach she bowed her diademed head tirelessly, her smile as gay and brilliant as the sun. The dignity of sovereignty was lightened and gladdened now with the affection which responded to that which she drew to her. All along that coloured river of the processional way, from stands and pavements and windows, from trees and housetops the happy tumult swept her to her palace.

The rain came again before the coach had carried her and her consort to their home, but nothing dimmed the loyal fervour of her welcome.

When the gates of the Palace were closed and the troops of her realm, her dominions, and colonies had passed on their proud way out of sight the crowds swept in a great surge towards the Palace. A great cheer swelled to the sky – it could have been heard a mile away – when the Queen, in her crown, with the Duke and their two children, came from the tall windows on to the balcony to see the R.A.F. fly-past.

As the aircraft swept and thundered overhead the Queen and her consort waved repeatedly to the waving and cheering crowd. On the balcony they were joined by Queen Elizabeth the Queen Mother, Princess Margaret, the Duke and Duchess of Gloucester, the Princess Royal, the Duchess of Kent with her children, and Princess Alice, Countess of Athlone. The Duke of Cornwall and his sister joined enthusiastically in the salutation to the crowd. The royal appearance on the balcony lasted for 10 minutes, the focus of a great and sustained outburst of loyalty, which continued long after the royal group had withdrawn.

The Times, June 3, 1953

Queen Elizabeth II during her coronation, holding the symbols of monarchy – the orb and sceptre.

HEAD
OF STATE

HER MAJESTY'S GOVERNMENTS
by Valentine Low

Despite the entertaining fantasy promulgated by Peter Morgan in his play *The Audience*, no one really knows what is discussed during the weekly meetings between the Queen and the prime minister. Plenty of people have asked, however. In the early days of her reign, when the Queen was in her twenties and Winston Churchill was more than half a century her senior, his private secretary Jock Colville noticed that as the two of them got to know each other, the meetings got longer and longer. "What do you talk about?" he asked the prime minister. "Oh, mostly racing," he replied.

For all Churchill's jocularity, it would be a mistake to suppose that the meetings were all gossip and small talk. She read her boxes and made sure she always knew what was going on. "The Queen," Edward Heath wrote, "is undoubtedly one of the best-informed people in the world."

Now on her 14th prime minister, the Queen still sees Boris Johnson – who had not been born when her fifth prime minister, Harold Wilson, came to power – once a week, the Covid-19 pandemic permitting. Inevitably, over the years the Queen has got on better with some of her prime ministers than others. One suspects, for example, that her relationship with David Cameron was not improved by his embarrassing indiscretion in revealing how she "purred" down the phone after hearing the result of the Scottish independence referendum.

Churchill adored her and always occupied a special place in her affections; the historian Ben Pimlott in his biography of the Queen described how the weekly meetings would take on an almost jaunty air. "The premier would arrive wearing a frock coat and top hat, with a gleam in his eye, and disappear happily into secret conclave."

Harold Macmillan treated their relationship as what Pimlott called a kind of "chivalrous fantasy", and she got on surprisingly well with Wilson (according to him), despite having little in common with him. He treated her as an equal and aides noted that their audiences grew longer over time. Wilson once described the meetings as the only times when he could have a serious conversation, which would not be leaked, with somebody who wasn't after his job.

Not all of the relationships have been quite so easy. When Heath first met her, he said: "I lost my nerve and said to her, 'Have you been busy lately, Ma'am?' 'That,' she replied, 'Is the sort of question lord mayors ask when I visit cities.'" It did not get much better after that. Heath had no small talk and little time for women, and as a member of the household observed, "the Queen found Heath hard going".

Politically too they were at odds: she was a fervent believer in the Commonwealth, while Heath was a passionate European to the exclusion of all else and did not think much of the Commonwealth. In 1971 he wanted her to stay away from the first Commonwealth leaders conference in Singapore because of the expected furious reaction to his plan to resume arms sales to South Africa; it took an intense meeting between monarch and prime minister at Balmoral for her to agree.

Even the most confident and socially adept of prime ministers could be put in their place. Recalling his first audience, Tony Blair said: "She was ... direct. 'You are my tenth prime minister. The first was Winston. That was before you were born.' I got a sense of my relative seniority, or lack of it."

The lack of warmth between the Queen and Margaret Thatcher has been well documented, if a little exaggerated. Over time, the Queen grew to respect Thatcher, who was a devoted monarchist; as one of her ministers observed, "no one would curtsy lower than Margaret".

While there may not have been animosity between the two women, there was a lack of mutual understanding. One story has it that the Queen said of her prime minister, in fond mock despair: "Mrs Thatcher never listens to a word I say." Thatcher, in turn, found some of the royal ways baffling, such as the Queen's habit of washing up after Balmoral barbecues with her bare hands. Famously, after one visit she sent her a pair of washing-up gloves.

In 1986, against a background of Thatcher riling some members of the Commonwealth by refusing to back sanctions against South Africa, *The Sunday Times* published a story saying that the Queen was dismayed by some of Thatcher's policies. This went beyond the Commonwealth crisis over South Africa, the paper said: "The Queen considers the prime minister's approach to be uncaring, confrontational and divisive."

The extent to which the Queen believed that is an issue that has long been argued over and not satisfactorily resolved. It is, however, an impression that has not gone away, although the biographer Hugo Vickers has argued that he knows for certain that the Queen was deeply upset by the way Thatcher was ousted in 1990 and immediately gave her the Order of Merit. Whatever their differences, there was always a respect between the women. When the Queen attended Thatcher's 80th birthday party as guest of honour, others were touched by the sight of the Queen taking Thatcher's hand as she raised her from a deep curtsy before guiding the frail former prime minister through the throng of assembled friends and admirers.

After Thatcher's death in 2013, the Queen broke with tradition to attend her funeral, the first time since the death of Churchill in 1965 that she had attended the funeral of a former prime minister. That, however, had been a state occasion; this was a personal choice, and one that Thatcher's family said would have left her "humbled".

As the Queen has grown older, and her prime ministers younger, their relationship has changed. When John Major – the first prime minister who was younger than the Queen – succeeded Thatcher, the Queen "discovered in him a more relaxed, congenial visitor than his predecessor", according to Pimlott.

David Cameron, whose brother used to go to tea at Windsor because he was at prep school with Prince Edward, revealed how she would occasionally tease him. Although she has not seen *The Audience*, she got wind of the scene in which she supposedly dozes off as Cameron bores her with the latest political machinations from Europe. Later, the (real) Queen told him that she had never fallen asleep during their weekly meetings. After a dramatic pause, she added: "Yet!"

Brexit inevitably dominated the short premiership of Theresa May, but whatever their respective personal views on the outcome of the referendum, the two women are said to have established a good rapport.

Of the Queen's relationship with Gordon Brown, almost nothing is known. However, he did provide one of the more amusing prime ministerial moments of her reign when he appeared to get lost at a state banquet at Windsor Castle after walking the wrong way round the banqueting table. "Has the prime minister got lost?" the Queen asked. "He disappeared the wrong way at the crucial moment."

While it is certain that the Queen has not shown the slightest inclination to interfere in politics, she found on a number of occasions that it was hard to avoid. During the Suez crisis of 1956 the Queen was in the invidious position of being kept thoroughly informed, thanks to a stream of Foreign Office papers and telegrams, so much so that she knew more of what was happening than a number of ministers, some of whom were notoriously kept in the dark. It also put her in a dilemma with regard to the Commonwealth: did she tell Commonwealth leaders what she had been told in confidence, or did she betray their trust by withholding information that was relevant to their interests?

As for the Queen's position on Anthony Eden's Suez intervention, it seems she was not entirely neutral. "I think the Queen believed Eden was mad," recalled one palace aide. While she may not have gone so far as to protest against the Suez operation, one courtier recalled: "She may have said to Eden something like, 'Are you sure you are being wise?'"

Overseas visits produced their share of dilemmas. In 1961 the Queen had been due to visit Ghana, where the newly independent country was starting to move towards single-party rule and dictatorship. With violence and anti-British feeling on the increase there were valid arguments for cancelling the visit, balanced by fears that to do so would drive Ghana into the arms of the Soviet Union. "She is grateful for concerns about her safety," Macmillan recorded in his diary, "but impatient of the attitude to treat her as a woman."

Determined to support the Commonwealth, the Queen went, and she danced at a state ball with the Ghanaian president. In South Africa a nationalist newspaper complained of "the honoured head of the once mighty British Empire dancing with black natives of pagan Africa"; the Ghanaian press hailed her as "the greatest socialist monarch in the world".

One of the most controversial episodes in the Queen's political life came during the resignation of Macmillan as prime minister in 1963. He had been thinking – and dithering – about stepping down for some time, and then was forced into action when he had to go into hospital for a prostate operation. This was before the days when the Conservative party elected its leaders; the new leader was supposed to emerge through soundings, although there was no agreed mechanism as to how the process should work.

The ever-devious Macmillan, meanwhile, despite still recovering from his operation, was determined to mastermind the changeover from his hospital bed. Chaos ensued, with the leading contenders jockeying for position, the cabinet divided, backbench MPs throwing in their two ha'p'orth, and Macmillan doing everything in his power to ensure that the obvious candidate – Rab Butler, the deputy prime minister – did not get the job.

Buckingham Palace did its best to stay out of the fray, which served only to prompt speculation about what the Queen would do. In the event, Macmillan managed to organise it so that within three quarters of an hour of his eventual resignation the Queen was at his hospital bedside for a farewell meeting. She asked him for his advice, he suggested that she call for Lord Home (who would relinquish his title to become Sir Alec Douglas-Home), and she agreed.

According to Pimlott, the advice was thoroughly unconstitutional, although it may have been what she wanted to hear. An aide told him: "When she got the advice to call Alec she thought, 'Thank God'. She loved Alec – he was an old friend. They talked about dogs and shooting together. They were both Scottish landowners, the same sort of people, like old school friends."

It was, in Pimlott's view, "the biggest political misjudgment of her reign", although other constitutional experts, such as Vernon Bogdanor, disagree. In *The Monarchy and the Constitution* he says she correctly took the most straightforward course and avoided getting involved in the internal politics of the Conservative party.

The controversy caused by the selection process led to a change in the rules of the Tory party. Thus, by the time the Queen faced another constitutionally tricky moment – the 2010 general election, which was widely expected not to produce a party with an overall majority – her private secretary had done a thorough job of laying the groundwork with the cabinet secretary to ensure that when it came to the post-election horse-trading to choose a prime minister, a clearly defined process had been set in place. She was not going to get caught out again.

The two women didn't always see eye to eye, but no one would curtsy to the Queen lower than Margaret Thatcher, who was a devoted monarchist.

John Major was the first prime minister who was younger than the Queen.
She found him "more relaxed" than Thatcher.

The Queen with Gordon Brown.

The Queen is said to believe that Anthony Eden, left, was "mad" for intervening in the Suez crisis and asked him: "Are you sure you are being wise?"

Fellow Scottish landowner Sir Alec Douglas-Home, pictured with his wife, Elizabeth, would talk about dogs and shooting with the monarch.

The Queen told Tony Blair, her tenth prime minister: "The first was Winston. That was before you were born."

*Harold Wilson said his audiences with the Queen were his only chance
of a serious conversation that would not be leaked.*

The Queen had a special bond with Winston Churchill, pictured here with his predecessor, Clement Attlee, and Attlee's wife, Violet.

The Queen is said to have teased David Cameron, here with his wife, Samantha, and the Duke of Edinburgh, that she hadn't fallen asleep in their meetings – yet.

THE QUIET DIPLOMAT
by Valentine Low

The Queen fulfils her international role in a way that no British sovereign has done before. From her first triumphant tour as Princess Elizabeth to the delicate diplomacy of the 2015 Chinese state visit, she has met many world leaders, and they have often been highly impressed.

She still works a unique brand of magic. When the Chinese president Xi Jinping visited Britain in 2015, the palace welcome was treated by China as the sort of affirmation they could get nowhere else in the world. It had been the same in Germany that summer when Angela Merkel abandoned a meeting on the Greek economy to spend more time with her guest. And the Queen may be one of the few people capable of making Donald (and Melania) Trump seem happy to share the limelight.

Even when she has been among the most stellar players on the international stage, the Queen has shown a quiet magnetism that has remained undiminished – to say nothing of a capacity to surprise. When she and Michelle Obama put their arms around each other at a Buckingham Palace reception, it showed the Queen to be warmer and more affectionate than some have supposed, and less bound by protocol than those who surround her. The bond forged between them paved the way for a successful state visit by President Obama two years later.

Some bonds are stronger than others. When Vladimir Putin visited in 2000, he had tea with the Queen at Windsor Castle – a relatively brief visit that did not, presumably, feature any hugs. Three years later the Russian president paid a state visit that was notable, among other things, for his being 15 minutes late for the ceremonial welcome.

One of her warmest relationships was with Nelson Mandela. The South African president is reported to have been one of the few people who got away with calling her Elizabeth; she called him Nelson. They got off to a good start long before he was elected president. Recently released from prison, Mandela had been invited to the 1991 Commonwealth summit in Harare but, because he was not a head of government, he had not been invited to the Queen's banquet. Her courtiers, unsure what to do, asked her. "Let's have him," she said. They got on, it was said, "like a house on fire".

Mandela even got the Queen to behave in unQueen-like ways. On his state visit to Britain in 1996 he asked for a concert at the Royal Albert Hall instead of a banquet. When, during the rousing finale, he got up to dance, she did likewise. "Good heavens," said one establishment figure. "The Queen is dancing!"

The Queen rides with Nelson Mandela, president of South Africa, in 1996. The two had a strong friendship and he is said to have been one of the few to be on first-name terms with the monarch.

The Queen with Vladimir Putin at Windsor Castle, 2000.

The Queen with the German chancellor Angela Merkel, 2009.

The Queen with President Barack Obama, 2011.

In an era when we are accustomed to the international celebrity status of the Duchess of Cambridge, and before her Diana, Princess of Wales, it is easy to forget that the young Elizabeth had a star quality at least as great, if not greater. Crowds came out in their thousands to see her, and statesmen found themselves falling for her charms. In a postwar world short of glamour and fun there was fanciful talk of the "Faerie Princess". Later, when youth and beauty were no longer the most important weapons in her armoury, she employed her wisdom and experience to useful effect. On more than one occasion the British government owed some of its foreign policy successes to the backstage diplomacy carried out unnoticed by the Queen.

She won her first international admirers before she became Queen. As Princess Elizabeth, she undertook a tour of Canada in 1951 that included a trip to the USA. President Truman was smitten. Afterwards the British ambassador, Sir Oliver Franks, wrote to the King to say that when Truman appeared with her in public he conveyed "the impression of a very proud uncle presenting his favourite niece to his friends". Truman himself said: "When I was a little boy, I read about a fairy princess, and there she is."

His successor, Dwight Eisenhower, became a firm friend. When the Eisenhowers were guests at Balmoral in 1959 he admired some home-made drop scones and she promised to send him the recipe. Later, she wrote to the president: "Seeing a picture of you in today's newspaper standing in front of a barbecue grilling quail reminded me that I had never sent you the recipe of the drop scones which I promised you at Balmoral. I now hasten to do so and I do hope you will find them successful." She concluded: "I think the mixture needs a great deal of beating while making and shouldn't stand around too long before cooking."

Even the Russians were won over. When Nikita Khrushchev visited Britain in 1956 the Communist party general secretary likened her to "the sort of young woman you'd be likely to meet walking along Gorky Street on a balmy summer afternoon".

When Britain was negotiating to enter what was then called the Common Market, it tried to overcome French objections by inviting General Charles de Gaulle for a state visit in 1960 to charm him into submission. He was given a ceremonial welcome and a state dinner and was delighted that all the royal family came to a banquet at the French embassy. He appreciated the Queen's fluency in French and realised, he wrote, that "she was well informed about everything, that her judgments, on people and events, were as clear-cut as they were thoughtful, that no one was more preoccupied by the cares and problems of our storm-tossed age". Unfortunately, de Gaulle still said "Non".

During her state visit to Morocco in 1980, after erratic behaviour from King Hassan II, including his failure to appear for a luncheon until 5pm, he pointed at Robert Fellowes, her assistant private secretary at the time, and said he was responsible for the "terrible muddle". The Queen rebuked him: "I'll thank you not to speak to my staff like that."

The Queen has had to put up with some fairly unsavoury guests. She was uncomfortable entertaining Nicolae Ceausescu, the Romanian leader, during his state visit in 1978; out walking her dogs in the gardens at Buckingham Palace, she hid behind a bush rather than converse with the dictator and his wife. She was most angry with President Mobutu of Zaire, who visited in 1973; his wife smuggled a small dog through customs and ordered it steak from the palace kitchens. The deputy master of the household was told: "Get that dog out of my house!" It was duly put on a plane to Brussels.

The Queen's one great advantage over most democratically elected leaders, and certainly all British statesmen, is that she has been around much longer than any of them. Her longevity proved useful in the Commonwealth crisis of 1979, when African leaders turned against Britain for what they saw as its failure to act against white-ruled Rhodesia.

The Queen with the Indian prime minister Indira Gandhi, 1983.

The Queen with Zimbabwe's president Robert Mugabe, 1994.

The Queen with President Bill Clinton, along with the First Lady Hillary Clinton and daughter Chelsea, 2000.

The Queen with US Secretary of State Hillary Clinton and the French president Nicolas Sarkozy, 2009.

The Queen with President Richard Nixon, Princess Anne and Prince Charles.

The Queen with the Polish president Lech Wałęsa, 1991.

The Queen with the Irish president Michael D Higgins, 2014.

As the former Commonwealth secretary general Sir Sonny Ramphal said: "Julius Nyerere [of Tanzania] and Kenneth Kaunda [of Zambia] and people like that from Africa were young men when she became Queen, making their way in political life. She knew them as young prime ministers and young presidents and so over many years they were friends."

The Commonwealth heads of government meeting in Lusaka, which Margaret Thatcher initially refused to attend, seemed set to be a disaster. "Britain was looked on with the greatest possible distrust," said a minister. Not the Queen, however; when she arrived the government-owned *Zambia Daily Mail* contrasted her "extraordinary loving heart" with Thatcher's lack of sympathy.

Sir William Heseltine, the Queen's deputy private secretary at the time, said that the Queen helped the foreign secretary, Lord Carrington, to win over Thatcher to his plan to persuade the conference that the Rhodesia question was best solved by Britain, not the Commonwealth.

As head of the Commonwealth, the Queen was seen as transcending national boundaries. Kaunda recalled a conversation in Lusaka: "She said, 'My friend, you and I should be careful. We are under the scrutiny of the British prime minister.' I looked up and Mrs Thatcher had her eyes fixed on us." Softened up by the Queen, Kaunda swept Thatcher on to the dancefloor after the opening banquet and the meeting ended with an agreement that led to the negotiations for the peaceful establishment of an independent Zimbabwe.

The Queen was brought into play during the Falklands crisis in 1982. Britain had American support for a military response to the invasion but it was important to strengthen the bond. During a stay at Windsor Castle Ronald Reagan found the Queen "charming, down-to-earth", and went riding with her. In a speech to parliament, he confirmed his backing for the UK over the Falklands.

In her eighties the Queen still played an important role. The success of her state visit to the Republic of Ireland in 2011, when she laid a wreath to fallen Irish nationalists, was a triumph of her brand of quiet diplomacy. In 2014 it was followed by a state visit by the Irish president, Michael D Higgins, during which she shook hands with Martin McGuinness at Windsor Castle.

The important work was, perhaps, done behind the scenes. However, for many it is those moments in Dublin and Windsor that will go down in history – and the way the Queen, as ever, played her role to perfection.

Guests listen to a speech by the Queen in honour of the president of Ireland, Michael D Higgins, at a state banquet in Windsor, April 8, 2014.

The Queen with Pope John Paul II, 1982.

The Queen with President Gerald Ford, 1976.

The Queen with Emperor Hirohito of Japan, 1975.

The Queen with President George W Bush, 2007.

The Queen with Emperor Haile Selassie of Ethiopia, 1954.

The Queen making a toast at a state dinner in San Francisco, in 1983, with US president Ronald Reagan. The two got on famously, with Reagan calling her "charming" and "down-to-earth".

54 COUNTRIES, 92 LANGUAGES: THE COMMONWEALTH

by Giles Whittell

At most of the Queen's public events, her subjects turn out in her honour. At several, however, it is the Queen who does the honouring, and each time the object of her respect will be the same – the Commonwealth.

No other institution except the monarchy itself bears the stamp of the Queen's personality as clearly as this sprawling collection of mainly English-speaking former colonies. It is not universally admired but in a sense it is her life's work. Its expansion has been her proudest accomplishment on the world stage, and it is no coincidence that most of its 54 member states are represented at her various birthday celebrations.

The Queen's role as head of the Commonwealth gives the lie to the notion that she is powerless. As leader of a vast group of nations with shared aspirations, she wields impressive power whether she likes it or not.

The Queen used this power most memorably in 2013 when, for only the second time in her reign, she did not attend the biennial Commonwealth Heads of Government meeting (CHOGM). The meeting took place in Colombo. The Sri Lankan capital was recovering from civil war and its government was under condemnation for the deaths of about 100,000 civilian Tamils.

Aides said the Queen's non-appearance was not political. What did not need saying was that she was not going to fly halfway round the world to tarnish the Commonwealth by shaking hands with an alleged mass murderer. The effect for President Rajapaksa of Sri Lanka was devastating. In her place the Queen sent her son, and Prince Charles, in his main speech, avoided all mention of the civil war. He ended with a plaintive appeal to the "family values" that the Commonwealth represented. It was an awkward moment. Charles spoke for himself and his mother, and the subset of Commonwealth countries that successfully espouse democracy.

Overlooked in the fuss was the extraordinary fact that the Commonwealth exists at all; that it has expanded to include not just former British imperial possessions, but parts of Francophone Africa and a former Portuguese colony; and that it is the only international body apart from the United Nations to straddle the rich-poor divide on a global scale. The Commonwealth is loose enough not to break apart when stresses build, but coherent enough to function. It represents two billion people – more than a quarter of the world's population. It promotes democratic ideals even if not all its members practise them.

The Queen has been committed to the notion of a global English-speaking body since she was a young woman. Her first tour of the Commonwealth as Queen started five months after her Coronation, covered 40,000 miles and lasted seven months. For her Silver Jubilee she went farther: 56,000 miles. At 76, she marked her Golden Jubilee with trips to Canada, Australia, New Zealand and Jamaica. With very few exceptions she has attended Commonwealth summits not as an observer but as an exceptionally diligent chairwoman. She has made a point of getting to know other leaders, the better to anticipate their moves and moods. She has given hundreds of gifts and accepted hundreds more, among them a totem pole and a canoe.

Her father, George VI, had not taken the idea of a durable successor to the empire seriously. As Richard Bourne, the former head of the Commonwealth Human Rights Group, puts it, running the Commonwealth "just wasn't as much fun as being emperor of India". The King's daughter was more concerned with duty than fun and understood that the Commonwealth had to be on the right side of history.

She had grave misgivings about Anthony Eden's bellicose response to the Suez crisis in 1956 and, according to her assistant private secretary at the time, may have gone as far as to remonstrate with him over his decision to retake the canal by force. She smoothed the path to Zimbabwe's independence, persuading Zambia's president Kenneth Kaunda to remove a potentially inflammatory reference to Robert Mugabe and Joshua Nkomo as "freedom fighters" from his speech at the Lusaka CHOGM in 1979.

Inspecting the troops of the Queen's Own Nigeria Regiment, Royal West African Frontier Force, which had been renamed in her honour before her visit in February 1956.

The Queen is greeted by children dressed in carnival costumes in Port of Spain, Trinidad, in 2009.

*Princess Margaret, who had a house on Mustique, welcomes the Queen
to the Caribbean island during her Silver Jubilee tour, 1977.*

The Queen and Prince Philip are entertained by Fijian traditional dancers on board the Royal Yacht Britannia, *1977.*

Visiting a wildlife park in Brisbane during her hugely successful tour of Australia, 2011.

At the Taj Mahal in Agra during a visit to India, 1961.

The Queen in India in 1961, admiring the fashions.

She lobbied behind the scenes for democracy and against military dictatorship in Nigeria, and where democracy took root, she did her best to help it flourish. In one case highlighted by historians she was able to prevail on Ghana's charismatic president Jerry Rawlings to stand down at the end of his term (in 2001) rather than follow the disastrous example of Africa's self-appointed presidents-for-life.

Most importantly and courageously, the Queen sided with justice and the Commonwealth against Britain's own Conservatives in the long struggle against South African apartheid. It seems unconscionable now that Edward Heath defended selling arms to South Africa on the grounds that they would not be used to enforce apartheid and Britain had an inalienable right to set its own trade policies. The Queen thought it unconscionable in 1971.

She consented with reluctance to Heath's demand that she should not attend that year's CHOGM in Singapore. The government tried to persuade her not to go to the next meeting either, in Canada, but she went anyway.

The rift between Buckingham Palace and Margaret Thatcher over South African sanctions was deep and enduring. Thatcher's refusal to back the embargo led to a broad boycott of the 1986 Commonwealth Games in a personal humiliation for the Queen. She continued to attend summits even so, including an especially difficult one in Limassol in 1993 when Greek Cypriots branded her a killer for Britain's hanging of nine anti-British rebels nearly four decades earlier.

By the early 1990s the Commonwealth was limping. It had split over South Africa, played no role in ending the Cold War and was sidelined by the Queen's own government as an annoying irrelevance for having the temerity to lecture Britain on its moral shortcomings when its members harboured plenty of their own.

Yet it survived. More than that, it thrived. Over the next 20 years South Africa rejoined after a 33-year suspension, and non-Anglophone developing countries started to apply for membership. For Cameroon and Mozambique it was granted in 1995; for Rwanda in 2009; and in 2020 the Maldives became its 54th member.

A 2011 report by the preposterously named Eminent Persons Group said the Commonwealth was drifting from its reformist mission and was hypocritical over human rights. Undaunted, the Queen urged it to dust itself down, respond to new challenges such as food insecurity and climate change, and "stay fit and fresh for tomorrow".

The same year, the Commonwealth had a long moment in the sun on the Queen's triumphant 11-day tour of Australia that took in Canberra, Brisbane and Melbourne. She opened that year's CHOGM in Perth, observing that such meetings' importance "has always been in precise relationship to their relevance". It was a neat, disarming touch. The theme of the summit was "women as agents of change" and she urged all to continue to strive together to promote the theme in a lasting way.

The Queen had been met at the start of the tour by Australia's first woman prime minister. Julia Gillard, an avowed Republican, had refused to curtsy and bowed awkwardly on the red carpet instead. Aides said the Queen "couldn't give two hoots". She swept all before her on her 16th visit to a country that has always reciprocated her affection. Before departing, she and Prince Philip were guests at a barbecue on Perth's Esplanade, attended by about 200,000 people.

Four years later, aged 89, the Queen resumed her role of leading the Commonwealth from the front. After the Colombo hiatus she took Prince Philip with her to host the heads of government in Malta. The trip was partly down memory lane, to a villa she had lived in before ascending the throne. But it was also the fulfilment of a duty to the Commonwealth she said she still cherished after more than 60 years.

The Commonwealth remains a popular and useful global forum – popular for the 4,500 athletes who competed in the 2018 Commonwealth Games, held on the Gold Coast, Queensland; useful for advocates such as Malala Yousafzai, shot in the head while going to school in Pakistan. The guest of honour at the 2014 Commonwealth Day service in London, Malala embodies the Commonwealth's ideals as well as the Queen herself.

Kenneth Kaunda, who was born in what was Northern Rhodesia in 1924, and lived on until 2021, once remarked that the transition from empire to Commonwealth was made possible by the Queen's personality. "Without that," he said, "many of us would have left."

The Queen with Kenneth Kaunda, 1979.

Touring a market in the British Virgin Islands, 1977.

QUEEN
AND COUNTRY

THE CROWN

by James Owen

Few Britons can remember when the Queen was not a part of their lives. Her own life and reign have been so long that the shadow of their span will touch centuries yet to come, even as they have been tinged by centuries past. The first prime minister to guide her, Winston Churchill, had been known in the late 19th century to her great-great-grandmother, Queen Victoria. The Queen's great-grandson, Prince George, whose time as sovereign will in some measure be shaped by her experiences, may still be King well into the 22nd century – nearly 100 years from now.

She grew up when the First World War was a recent memory. As a young woman, she lived through the Second World War, and as Queen she has seen all the great events that have shaped modern Britain, from the Beatles to Brexit. The early years of the NHS, the end of austerity (the first time around), the Cambridge spies and the Profumo scandal, the Troubles in Northern Ireland, the Falklands War, the Iraq War, joining (and leaving) Europe, terrorist atrocities, "test tube babies", even a World Cup triumph at Wembley – she has been here for all of it.

Motorways arrived, shillings went and the death penalty was abolished. A boy she saw playing a rabbit in a school play, David Cameron, grew up to become her 12th prime minister (before leaving to spend more time in his shepherd's hut).

She celebrated her first quarter of a century on the throne long before anybody began to carry around their own computers, let alone ones that made telephone calls. And her reign has now been long enough for her to watch it dramatised as history in the TV series *The Crown*.

Above all, she has seen Britain's conception of itself change beyond recognition. The still substantial empire that she inherited has gone its own way, and the events of the Suez crisis in 1956 ended the pretence that the country was still a great world power.

Gone, too, is much of the class deference that underpinned the monarchy's role as the pinnacle of society. With the changes have come more scrutiny and different expectations, altering steadily but fundamentally the Queen's relationship with her subjects.

In truth, the nature of the monarchy had already assumed a radically new shape following the event which made her heir to the throne. Amid its personal drama, what the abdication of her uncle, Edward VIII, really signalled was that whoever was sovereign accepted that they could not do as they pleased. Their task was to keep the country united, not to cause division. Duty trumped desire, even happiness – a lesson that the young Elizabeth took to heart.

By the time of her Coronation in 1953, the belief that hers must be a participatory monarchy was confirmed by the decision, reluctantly taken under pressure from public opinion, to televise the ceremony. Nevertheless, the Queen vetoed filming of the sacred moments when she was anointed and crowned.

Almost of equal significance, however, was the moment a few hours later when the press spotted Princess Margaret tenderly picking fluff from the jacket of Peter Townsend, the royal equerry with whom she was secretly in love.

The furore that ensued, as the Palace and the public grappled with the consequences of a member of the royal family marrying someone who was divorced, marked the start of a new approach by the media to the Queen and her relations, focusing on their behaviour as individuals. It was a change in emphasis to which the Queen was slow to adapt.

Not a natural seeker of the spotlight – unlike Margaret – the Queen is instinctively conservative and particularly during the first part of her reign she heeded the advice of courtiers who shared her caution. This "safety first" approach meant that she rarely erred. Despite the social changes and conflict that Britain has witnessed in 70 years, hardly ever, for example, has she expressed an opinion about politics that might have stirred up resentment.

Only once, according to her former private secretary Martin Charteris, did she feel that she had put a foot wrong. In October 1966, a spoil tip from a Welsh colliery, loosened by weight of rainwater, slid down onto the village of Aberfan below. The disaster claimed 144 lives, of whom 116 were children, most buried under the avalanche of mud that engulfed the local junior school. Many of their parents were miners who ran from the coalface to dig for survivors, largely in vain.

Although Prince Philip went to the site soon after, it was not until eight days later that the Queen herself visited it. Advisers had suggested that she go before but she had felt that her presence might detract attention from the rescue efforts. Her assistant press secretary at the time, William Heseltine, later said that in hindsight she thought that she ought to have gone there earlier. "It was a sort of lesson to us," he observed, "that you need to show sympathy and to be there on the spot, which I think people craved from her." Aberfan was one of the few occasions on which the Queen showed emotion in public, trying to hold back tears.

The documentary *Royal Family*, which aired in 1969, went further still in penetrating the façade. Commentators at the time fretted that it "let daylight in", removing any mystique that still clung to the Queen. Its revelation, however, that in private she and her children led lives not so different from many middle-class families began to reduce what appearance of distance from them there remained.

Yet what in the long run the public seemed to want was a fuller appreciation by the monarchy of what that distance should signify. The Queen has been famous since she was born. Anne Frank kept pictures of the "little princesses" on the walls of her wartime hiding place in Amsterdam.

The Queen and Prince Philip visiting Aberfan, October 29, 1966.

When she became Princess of Wales in 1981, Lady Diana Spencer was less used to that status, and less schooled in how it should be worn. Although she undoubtedly revelled in the attention that she drew, what people responded to was someone who looked royal but also openly empathised with the struggles of others. Nearer to a modern celebrity than a traditional royal, Diana had star power yet did not feel out of reach.

That impression was perhaps reinforced by the very public airing of her travails, with the Palace's muted response seeming old-fashioned by comparison. Another lesson had to be learnt in the aftermath of Diana's death in 1997, when the Queen's own wish was to remain at Balmoral to allow Prince William and Prince Harry to grieve in private.

Yet the mood in the country turned from shock at Diana's death to dismay as the Palace's lack of official response to it appeared chilly and unfeeling. For perhaps the only time in her reign, the Queen's hand, as the historian Hugo Vickers put it, was forced. She felt obliged to return to London to see the thousands of floral tributes left by the public for Diana and to make a live television address acknowledging the feelings of those who had laid them.

She described Diana as "an exceptional and gifted human being", and told the nation that she was speaking to them not just as their Queen but "as a grandmother" (a humanising touch added to her draft by Alastair Campbell, a journalist before he became adviser to the prime minister, Tony Blair).

Almost 70 years on from her Coronation, the two institutions central to the ceremony, and at the time to the British way of life, have had to renegotiate in an unprecedented fashion their relationship with those over whom they once held sway. The Church of England has undoubtedly struggled to find ways of remaining such a relevant presence in people's lives.

The Crown, perhaps more easily able to adapt its raison d'être, has succeeded better, especially in the two decades after Diana's death. Notable triumphs include the steep rise in public affection for the Duchess of Cornwall, once reviled as the "other woman" in Prince Charles's marriage, and the sight of one of his sons marrying a divorced woman of mixed race, Meghan Markle.

Whatever difficulties may lie in the future, much of the credit for the affection in which the monarchy is still widely held is due to the Queen's resilience – a word that means not only tough but flexible. One only has to look to the royal houses of Spain or Belgium, among others, to see failures of judgement by her contemporaries that have gravely damaged their standing. The challenges that her successors face will be different from those she met, yet if the House of Windsor is to continue to thrive, they too will have to move with the times.

The Queen and Prince Philip arrive at the Chapel Royal to pay their respects to Diana, Princess of Wales, September 5, 1997, the day before her funeral.

Peace Returns to Aberfan, Villagers Moved by Queen's Visit

Aberfan is quiet. The great black tip that crushed Pantglas school is no longer the scene of feverish activity. With only a few workers of one contracting firm at the site, there is little to tell the tale of the past nine days.

There are still scores of police, but the faces have changed; uniforms are clean and bright and there is no weariness in their eyes. The villagers are getting used to the many strangers.

I spoke to some villagers today. Two things, they say, will never be forgotten – the terror of October 21 and the "kindness and sympathy" of the Queen who visited them yesterday.

The visit, as Mr. T. Griffiths, Chief Constable of Merthyr Tydfil, said on Friday, was to the people of Aberfan. "There will be no glory or royal glamour to this visit", he said. He was right. No cheers or flag waving welcomed the Queen and Duke of Edinburgh. The loudest noise was the sober choruses of "goodbye."

A young woman Red Cross worker told me today that it had been an almost painful sight. "The Queen seemed so near tears but she kept fighting them back. We all felt very close to her", she said.

While the royal couple were always surrounded by quiet villagers as they walked through the streets of Aberfan there was no pushing or jostling. The Queen stopped often to talk to those bereaved.

Councillor J. Williams and his wife Beatrice, who lost seven relatives in the disaster, were host to the visitors for 20 minutes. Tea was served in the front room of the Williams's home and the tragedy was explained.

The Queen appeared most moved as she accepted a small posy of flowers from Karen Jones, aged three. The posy was inscribed "From the remaining children of Aberfan".

The Times, October 30, 1966

The Queen and Prince Philip visit the coal-mining village of Aberfan following the disaster that resulted in the deaths of 116 children and 28 adults.

THE ROYAL GARDEN PARTY
by Daniel Finkelstein

"We do these things very well," my grandmother used to say when I was a boy and we watched a royal event on television. I thought it was a fitting comment; it seemed to me true, as far as I could make out from the telly, and I took pride in it.

Yet looking back, I think the most interesting word in the sentence was "we". My grandmother was born in Poland, as was my father. My mum was born in Berlin and brought up in Amsterdam. So it is interesting that the word "we" came naturally.

I think of King John as being part of my history, even though around the time of Magna Carta, my family was celebrating the crowning of Daniel of Galicia as King of Halych-Volhynia – give or take a hundred years or so.

I think this is part of the Queen's achievement, and her importance. She has somehow made a diverse people – with an incredibly varied history – think of themselves as "we".

The royal garden party is one of the things my grandmother was talking about when she praised how we do things. I didn't experience it on television, however. I went.

It is almost 25 years ago now, while I was working for Conservative Central Office. I knew I hadn't been selected to go because of any special distinction. The office got some invitations and it was my turn. Still, it was nice to get the stiff, embossed card from the Lord Chamberlain. And I would definitely have put it on the mantelpiece if we'd had one. As it was, I left it nonchalantly on the radiator shelf, face up, just in case anyone came to mend the radiator and might be so impressed that they mended it more carefully.

When my wife and I arrived at Buckingham Palace, there was a queue to get in. Quite a long one. This was due to something I should have realised earlier. Indeed, I probably knew it, if I had been bothered to think it through.

Each party has many thousands of guests. About 8,000 each. Of course they do, or I would not have been invited.

However obvious and necessary this may be, it does, at first, seem a little disappointing. Yet as it turns out, it isn't a disappointing event. How could it be? Even walking across the gravel at the palace was exciting.

In order for a garden party to be anything other than a scrum, it has to be carefully organised. And fortunately, it is. Guests are encouraged to stand in lanes and a number are selected to meet members of the royal family. We were not, but because the Queen was meeting someone very close to where we were standing, we felt included in the conversation.

It was quite cleverly done. The whole royal family were present – the Queen Mother, for instance, was there – so you felt part of a special occasion, despite the number of guests. And after the lanes and collecting tea you could stroll round the gardens, which meant you weren't standing in a crowd the whole time.

Watching the Queen work is fascinating. Each encounter is a highlight in the life of the person she is meeting, while, for her, being just a few moments in the schedule.

These are moments the visitor will never forget and she won't remember even by suppertime. She has to do the same things, say the same things, over and over again.

Yet it never seems like that. She is supremely professional, warm without being less than regal, interested without exhausting herself with small talk. I feel very fortunate to have been invited. The sense of being "we" is strong within me.

A garden party at the Palace in 2012. About 8,000 guests attend each event.

FIT FOR A QUEEN
by Anna Murphy

"If I wore beige," the Queen once said, "nobody would know who I am." Dressed head to toe in cerise or turquoise, on the other hand, and there is no question as to who One might be, no difficulty in picking One out in a crowd.

At heart Her Majesty's sartorial choices are the regal equivalent of the hi-vis jacket, and often almost as bright. (Sunshine yellow has been a favourite shade since the 1980s.)

The Queen has made up her own sartorial rulebook. She has had to; it's not as if there had been a recent precedent for a female British head of state when she succeeded her father in 1952. (And nor will there be a subsequent one; the next three in line to the throne are male.)

Aside from her adherence to colour, she has strong views on hats, for example; above all that she should wear one, but also that the brim should be off the face so as not to inhibit her public getting a clear sightline. She is all about her audience after all.

What else? She likes a two-inch block heel on her shoes (by Anello & Davide) to add height to her 5ft 4in stature without sacrificing comfort. And her boxy patent bags (by Launer) are made with a slightly longer handle so they can be hooked over her forearm without catching on her cuff. Everything she wears, or carries, is custom made; the Queen leaves the high street to the Duchess of Cambridge, thank you very much. No playing the everywoman for her.

The Queen has never seen fashion as a leveller; quite the reverse. Take her 1947 wedding dress, for example. What would be the embattled public's response to her extravagant seed-pearl-and-crystal-encrusted Norman Hartnell confection? Not horror, as some feared, but delight at their twinkly fairytale princess amid all that drear.

Sunshine yellow has been one of the Queen's favourite colours for decades.

On less formal occasions the Queen has always preferred clothes that are more practical for her favourite pastimes, such as walking and riding.

It was Hartnell she called on again to make her Coronation dress six years later, insisting that the floral symbols of Great Britain and the Commonwealth be incorporated, from Irish shamrocks to Canadian maple leaves. Those shamrocks reappeared – 2,091 of them this time – embroidered on the robe she wore during her historic 2011 visit to Ireland. On royal tours the Queen has consistently used her clothes to honour her host country.

How could anyone who became monarch the moment a crown was put on her head ignore the semantics of dress? Indeed, so emblematic has the Queen's mode of attire become over the years that you can see its influence on other women in the public eye, from Margaret Thatcher to Hillary Clinton (the former even co-opted those Launer handbags, and loved a hat). We don't only recognise our Queen from her head on our stamps but from her signature ensembles.

Like the good daughter she was, the young Elizabeth used her mother's favourite designer, Hartnell, during early adulthood. However, once she became Queen, she began working with him to develop a different look, eschewing her mother's fussy school-of-Barbara-Cartland chiffons in favour of sleeker lines. She was a woman in a man's world and she needed to dress to be taken seriously, while still signalling her femininity.

She also came to rely upon Hardy Amies, who was celebrated for his subtle re-toolings of Parisian trends – think couture with added stiff upper lip. In more recent years the majority of the Queen's wardrobe has been created by Angela Kelly, who has served as her senior dresser since 2002. The daughter of a Liverpool dock worker, Kelly is also the Queen's personal assistant and close confidante.

Away from the public eye the Queen has never needed any help getting dressed. She wears clothes that don't get in the way of walking and riding: tweed skirts, lace-up brown shoes, sensible woollies, a headscarf, assorted hardcore varieties of raincoat. (She's Queen of the notoriously drizzly British Isles after all.) The colours she chooses are those of our country, her country: earth, moss, heather, lichen. She wears a kind of camouflage. In her private life she can, at last, blend in.

The purples and blues.

The turquoises and greens.

The yellows and golds.

The oranges and pinks.

Hats ...

... and more hats.

The casual outfits.

The gowns.

RULING
PASSIONS

THE QUEEN AT HOME
by Hugo Vickers

At state banquets the goldplate comes out. The Queen has been known to point out to state visitors that she does not live like that every day. In contrast, the Queen lives simply, even if on the outskirts of considerable grandeur. She enjoys pleasures such as walking and feeding her dogs, and riding in the grounds at Windsor, Sandringham and Balmoral. Unlike Queen Elizabeth the Queen Mother, she is not personally extravagant.

She divides her time between four royal residences: Buckingham Palace, her official residence and what can be considered the monarch's main office; Windsor Castle, where she weekends in the Victorian Tower overlooking acres of garden, distant fields and woodland, and where she and Prince Philip shielded during the pandemic; Sandringham, the sprawling Edwardian mansion that is the place for Christmas and where the stud is based; and Balmoral, her gothic Victorian Scottish residence, the place for summers in the Highlands – and for the August weekend visit from the prime minister and his wife.

At the palace, the Queen occupies – as during his lifetime did the Duke of Edinburgh – a long corridor on the Constitution Hill side of the building. The place has the feel of a rather grand Edwardian hotel. The duke, whose rooms once belonged to King George VI, had a library, a large drawing room, a smaller study, his bedroom and a bathroom.

The Queen's rooms were formerly used by her mother: an audience room, where she receives formal visitors in some style, followed by her dining room where she dines if she doesn't have an official engagement, a study sitting room (with a bow window), bedroom and dressing room. When the Queen is in her rooms, a page stands outside the door.

We get occasional glimpses of the Queen in her private surroundings when she records her Christmas broadcast to the Commonwealth. Her rooms are

On the sofa with a corgi in 1969, in a still taken by Joan Williams during the making of the BBC film Royal Family.

formal and grand with fine furniture and paintings, and on every table there are photographs of her children, grandchildren and great grandchildren, alongside signed photographs of foreign monarchs, many of them cousins. She has a private entrance into the garden, where footmen can be spotted walking the corgis, when she cannot do that herself. She can also emerge from her rooms into the state rooms along the garden side of the palace, through a mirror door, which swings open so she is suddenly there.

At Windsor Castle the Queen's private apartments, where she can make her own breakfast, overlook the Long Walk. She likes to ride her pony and walk her dogs in the Home Park. The Countess of Wessex and her children often ride with her. On Sundays she drives herself to morning service in the Royal Chapel at Royal Lodge and sometimes goes for post-matin drinks, for instance, before her death in 2016, with Margaret Rhodes, her cousin, or to another home in the park, such as the deputy ranger's.

At Easter, there is the Easter Court, when the Queen stays at the castle for about three weeks. Guests – often the heads of charities or leading lights in their field – are invited to what is known as a "dine and sleep". They are shown to their rooms where their suitcases are unpacked. The Queen presides at a dinner party and afterwards there is often a tour of the royal library, where items will have been brought out, according to their interests. They say goodbye at the end of the evening. They don't see her again the next morning and they leave after breakfast.

The Queen spends the week after her official birthday in June at Windsor and, after entertaining the Knights and Ladies of the Garter on the Monday, she spends five days at Royal Ascot. Although this has a formal side with a carriage procession, she does not consider it a public duty: it is a pleasure. As such, it is perhaps the only occasion when, to some extent, she politely ignores other racegoers. Her interest is the horses.

For the Christmas break and occasionally in the summer she goes to Sandringham. Here the atmosphere is similar to many country houses owned by the aristocracy – life is directed towards the outdoors.

The Queen takes her summer holiday at Balmoral between July and October. Local landowners are invited to dinner and there is a succession of house guests – mainly family friends and relatives.

The Queen drives visitors around the estate in her Land Rover, or treats them to the traditional royal family "cook out". The duke used to conduct proceedings on a specially designed barbecue, which travelled in a trailer behind a Land Rover, with food and drink in compartments. It meant that the royal family could dispense with staff; the Queen liked to do the washing-up herself on these occasions.

The prime minister and his wife are invited for a night at Balmoral at the end of August. This tends to coincide with the Braemar Games on the Saturday and a visit to Crathie church on the Sunday, at which the prime minister might read a lesson. A key event is the private audience with the Queen in her informal sitting room. Other than that, the visiting PM is expected to merge into the royal family's life, accompanying the Queen on a stroll around the kitchen garden, or perhaps visiting the Prince of Wales at Birkhall.

Entertaining prime ministers is a variable feast for the Queen, with stories that have become the stuff of legend. Mrs Thatcher apparently tried to take over the washing-up after a barbecue. The Queen Mother happened to see Tony Blair and his wife arrive one year. Cherie was reluctant to curtsy, and the Queen Mother was heard to say: "Stiff knees, stiff knees." On the other hand, Gordon Brown was a more easy-going guest than his public persona would suggest.

Meanwhile, David Cameron recalled in his memoir how his visit to Balmoral was overshadowed by newspaper headlines at breakfast predicting that Scotland would vote to break up the Union, in the forthcoming referendum that Cameron himself had authorised.

The Queen and Prince Philip with their children at Sandringham in 1969,
from left: Edward, Anne, Charles and Andrew.

When at Balmoral the Queen usually wears tartan.
Here, she welcomes General Sir Peter Cosgrove, the Governor-General of Australia, to Balmoral Castle.

A QUEEN'S BEST FRIENDS
by Valentine Low

The Queen's corgis are an instantly recognisable part of her public image. From newspaper cartoons to the video she made with Daniel Craig for the 2012 London Olympics – in which the corgi Monty made a cameo appearance – when a corgi appears, the Queen is never far behind. They even play a crucial role in kickstarting the plot in Alan Bennett's literary fantasy about the Queen, *The Uncommon Reader.*

Yet for all the Queen's devotion to her corgis – and her dorgis, a cross between a dachshund and a corgi – it would be wrong to think that she is a one-breed woman. There are labradors too, and spaniels: the Queen takes an active interest in the Sandringham kennels, and in her prime was regarded as a highly proficient handler of gundogs.

Her first dog, however, the one that inspired her love of animals, was none of these; it was a cairn terrier, given to her by her uncle, the Prince of Wales, the future Edward VIII. Princess Elizabeth was three years old at the time.

The first corgi to enter her life was called Dookie, bought by her father, George Vl, in 1933. Others followed, generation after generation of them; one of the most notable was Susan, the matriarch of the dynasty. On the Queen's wedding day, when she and Prince Philip were driven in an open carriage from Buckingham Palace to Waterloo station for the start of their honeymoon, Susan travelled with them, snuggled up under a rug. At Waterloo she stole the show by tumbling out first on to the red carpet that awaited them.

Being a royal pet is, naturally, not a life short of privilege. At Buckingham Palace the dogs sleep in their own room, in wicker baskets raised a few inches off the floor to avoid draughts. Whenever she can, the Queen exercises them herself, and it is said that if she is wearing a headscarf when she comes into a room they sense that a walk is imminent and will scamper about excitedly.

The former royal chef Darren McGrady, who worked for the Queen for 11 years, once described how the corgis would be served only the finest fare. "One day it would be chuck steak, which we boiled and served with finely chopped, boiled cabbage and white rice. The next they'd have poached chicken or liver. Or rabbits shot by William or Harry that we'd clean, cook, debone and chop for the dogs."

If the dogs could be unruly, it seemed to be just the way the Queen liked it. "They chase rabbits like mad," the Queen's cousin Margaret Rhodes said once. "There are a lot of rabbits around Balmoral, certainly, and the Queen gets excited with the dogs chasing the rabbits, egging them on. Telling them to keep going – 'Keep on going!'" There could be trouble, though. Susan once bit the royal clock winder, and also attacked one of the palace sentries. Another dog bit a policeman.

There have been reports in recent years that the Queen was starting not to replace her dogs as they died. Monty Roberts, an informal adviser to the Queen, said in 2014 that she had declined his offer to find a puppy after the death of Monty. He told *Vanity Fair* magazine: "She didn't want any more young dogs. She didn't want to leave any young dog behind. She wanted to put an end to it."

While Prince Philip was ill in hospital in 2021, however, she was given a pair of puppies by Prince Andrew. She apparently viewed Muick and Fergus – named for her mother's brother, who was killed in the First World War – as a welcome distraction, particularly once she was grieving for her husband. Unhappily, Fergus died shortly after as well, but she still walks Muick, a corgi, together with another dorgi, Candy.

Princess Elizabeth and Princess Margaret with the dogs in the Little House – their two-thirds size cottage in the grounds of the Royal Lodge, Windsor – in 1936.

Queen Elizabeth walking the dogs on the Balmoral estate, along with Prince Philip, Princess Anne and Prince Charles.

The Queen at the Royal Windsor Horse Show, 1973.

The Queen chats to one of her pets on her return from Balmoral in 1986.

The Queen arrives at Aberdeen airport with a trio of dogs, ready to start her holiday in Balmoral in 1974.

SPORT OF QUEENS
by Julian Muscat

On the morning of her Coronation, Princess Elizabeth was asked by a lady-in-waiting how she was feeling. She replied that she was very well: her trainer had just called to relate that her horse Aureole had completed his Derby preparation with a pleasing gallop.

Four days later, on her first visit to Epsom, she watched in a state of high excitement as Aureole finished runner-up to Pinza. Aureole's noble effort is still the closest she has come to winning the Derby. Her inaugural win in a Classic would come four years later, her homebred filly Carrozza taking the Oaks at Epsom, ridden by Lester Piggott.

The Queen's relationship with racing is not so much a casual acquaintance as a full-blooded embrace. Racecourses are her sanctuary, where she can be herself. She is often at Newbury's spring meeting in April, when she is in her element. Unlike the Derby or Ascot, where she is invariably a focal point, here the Queen will simply dissolve into the mix. She moves around without overt security. She can be like any other owner as she assesses runners in the paddock before making her way through crowds towards the grandstand. During her visits to the races the Queen radiates happiness, in contrast to her oft-sombre appearance in the line of duty.

She would doubtless have spent more time on the racecourse if circumstances had permitted. She once mused that but for the Archbishop of Canterbury she would have been off in her plane every Sunday to Longchamp, in Paris, where her filly Highclere galloped to victory in the 1974 Prix de Diane.

If her zest for racing is plain, she reveals more about herself when visiting her horses at her trainers' stables. She wants no fuss; she wants only to see her thoroughbreds going through their paces. Her insistence on informality encourages her trainers to treat her in kind. Most of them do just that – especially Richard Hannon, who served her for 16 years until his retirement in 2013, and whose jovial insouciance the Queen found particularly amusing.

On one occasion, when Hannon tried to communicate with a rider recently arrived from India who understood no English, he turned to the Queen in exasperation and asked whether she could speak "Indian". When she replied that she couldn't, Hannon rejoined: "Well you ought to, Ma'am. You ruled the place for long enough."

Her love of racing surfaces spontaneously, as it did in 2008, when her horse Free Agent ended a nine-year royal drought at Ascot. There the Queen stood, punching the air before hot-footing it down to the winner's enclosure. "It was as if she was 20 years old," recalled her bloodstock and racing adviser John Warren, who succeeded his father-in law, the 7th Earl of Carnarvon, to the post on the latter's death in 2001. "The rest of us were struggling to keep up."

Warren is well placed to amplify the Queen's passion. "It didn't take me long to realise that her fundamental interest revolves utterly and totally around the horse itself," he said. "The depth of her knowledge is extraordinary. Nobody else in the country has been breeding racehorses for more than 60 years."

Princess Elizabeth was three years old when George V regaled his granddaughter with the story of Scuttle carrying the royal silks to victory in the 1928 One Thousand Guineas at Newmarket. A year later she was given Peggy, her first pony. However, her love of racing escalated in 1942, when her father owned a pair of superior racehorses whose exploits would bring him the accolade of Britain's leading owner.

In the spring of that year George VI took his daughter to Fred Darling's stables in Beckhampton, Wiltshire, to cast her eye over Big Game and Sun Chariot. The two horses would win four of the five Classics and Princess Elizabeth, then 16, was so smitten on touching their silken coats that she would not wash her hands for hours afterwards.

The Queen with her horse, Estimate, who galloped to victory in the Gold Cup of 2013 at Royal Ascot.

To the public, the Queen will always be synonymous with Royal Ascot. She hosts a lunch at Windsor Castle on each of the meeting's five days and is always anxious to arrive at the racecourse punctually. She has savoured 24 Royal Ascot winners in the distinctive purple and red royal silks, among them Expansive in the 1979 Ribblesdale Stakes, a race Her Majesty has won three times.

They came thick and fast in the early years, when the Royal Studs were not in competition with the plethora of Middle Eastern potentates who have patronised British racing since the early 1980s. There are limits to what she can spend on bloodstock: the royal horses are all paid for from the Queen's private purse. Nevertheless, despite front-line successes becoming increasingly elusive, the Queen's interest has intensified with the passing years.

In her early eighties she decided to overhaul bloodlines within the Royal Studs, a decision which in time led to fresh conquests. For the Queen, however, it is not all about the big occasion. It is about giving every one of her horses the best possible opportunity to express its potential.

Her biggest triumph to date came in 2013 when Estimate galloped away with Royal Ascot's signature race, the Gold Cup. It marked the first victory for a British monarch in the race's 207-year history, after which the Queen revealed that it was the race she had yearned to win above all others.

The Queen leads in her filly Carrozza after it won the Oaks at Epsom in 1957, ridden by Lester Piggott.

Congratulating her horse Expansive, which won the Ribblesdale Stakes at Ascot in 1979, with Lord Carnarvon (right).

With her racing manager John Warren on Derby Day at Epsom in 2012,
the first day of her four-day Diamond Jubilee celebrations.

With Ryan Moore, who rode the Queen's horse Estimate to victory in the Gold Cup at Ascot in 2013.

A
FAMILY AFFAIR

THE ROYAL TRIUMVIRATE

by Hugo Vickers

No women were closer to the Queen than her mother and sister. At first they had been a family of four – King George VI, Queen Elizabeth and the two princesses. The King was concerned that the "us four" arrangement would end when Princess Elizabeth married Prince Philip in 1947 as, inevitably, it did.

The dynamics changed again when the King died in 1952. The Queen Mother had been virtually acting head of state while the King had been gravely ill. Now she was to change from being a supporting wife to leading life on her own terms – a mixture of the diplomatic, ambassadorial and social.

Throughout her life, however, she remained a quiet force behind the Queen. They talked regularly on the telephone, they went to church at weekends in Windsor, she stayed in the castle for Ascot week and spent time with her daughter at Sandringham. The Queen deferred to her mother in many ways on private family occasions – for example, giving her the King's seat in the chapel at Royal Lodge (in Windsor Great Park) for Sunday matins.

She always allowed her mother a BAE 146 aircraft to travel in if she needed it, while this privilege was not automatically granted to Princess Margaret or to other members of the royal family. She did not rein in her mother's perceived extravagances, the Queen Mother believing that she should continue to occupy four residences – Clarence House in London, Royal Lodge, Birkhall on the Balmoral estate and the privately owned Castle of Mey in Thurso, in the far north of Scotland. At all of them she entertained extensively.

The Queen continued to run royal life much as in her father's day, out of respect for his memory and to please her mother. Inevitably changes had to be gradually introduced. It was always hinted that the royal family might give up Sandringham, their country estate in Norfolk, but that the Queen Mother would never have approved.

As the Queen Mother reached extreme old age, there is no doubt that she caused the Queen considerable worry by refusing to slow down. The Queen bought her a mobility buggy, decorated in her racing colours, but for some years the Queen Mother refused to use it. At the end of a ball to celebrate her golden wedding in 1997, the Queen was heard to say: "I'm trying to persuade Mummy to go to bed." The Queen Mother was 97 at the time. While the public looked on admiringly as the Queen Mother walked the length of the aisle of St Paul's Cathedral at the age of 100, the Queen was anxious that her mother might fall in public.

The death of the Queen Mother in March 2002, at the age of 101, while the cause of sorrow and reflection, also relieved the Queen of considerable stress. As she undertook her Golden Jubilee engagements, she looked more relaxed, began to dress more stylishly, and in a sense asserted her personality in a new way. For many years, the Queen Mother had drawn the affection of the nation to her by her outgoing and generous personality. Only in 2002 did the Queen herself finally, albeit quietly, assume the role of royal matriarch.

The Queen was also very close to Princess Margaret and was frequently concerned about her sister's happiness. They had spent their childhood together, been inseparable during the war and only slightly distanced by the Queen's marriage in 1947.

Margaret Whitlam, the wife of the Australian prime minister, Gough Whitlam, stayed at Windsor Castle in April 1973 and captured something of the relationship between the Queen and Princess Margaret: "You would have loved the sight of the sisters sitting side by side on the deep-piled cream sheepskin rug we gave Her Majesty for her birthday. They looked like 'the Little Princesses' on either one's teenage birthday." She also recorded that the Queen and her sister indulged in proficient imitations – "gentle send-ups" – of people around them, including the Queen Mother.

There were many occasions on which the Queen's public position as monarch clashed with her private feelings. As early as 1953 there was the question of Princess Margaret marrying a divorced equerry, Group Captain Peter Townsend, a man much liked by the Queen and by the Queen Mother. The Queen's private hopes for her sister's happiness were thrown into conflict with her role as head of the Church of England, which at that time was sternly hostile to divorce.

Princess Margaret did not have her mother's resilience. Whereas the Queen Mother never disappointed the British public, Princess Margaret was more capricious. She did not aim to please and win over people in the way the Queen Mother did. The royal family were surprised when Princess Margaret married Antony Armstrong-Jones (later Viscount Snowdon), a photographer, in 1960.

The marriage was happy at first but ultimately unravelled. Their separation in 1976 and divorce in 1978 was a time of great sadness and upheaval in Princess Margaret's life and she received the Queen's moral support. In the mid-1990s, Princess Margaret's life settled on to a more even keel with the marriages of her children and the arrival of grandchildren, but then her health broke down.

Devoted as the Queen was to her mother and sister, their deaths, within a few weeks of each other in 2002, released her from pressure and anxiety. Inevitably, she minded Princess Margaret's death more. She had been the companion of her childhood, four years younger, and she missed a forceful, animated and spirited person.

Princess Margaret and Princess Elizabeth playing with the family dogs.

The Queen Mother – pictured here with Princess Margaret and the Queen – refused to slow down in her old age.

The Queen celebrates the Queen Mother's 80th birthday with Princess Margaret on August 4, 1980.

THE QUEEN'S CHILDREN
by Sally Bedell Smith

When she became Queen at the age of 25, Elizabeth was already the mother of three-year-old Prince Charles and 18-month-old Princess Anne. Her one maternal adjustment to what had been her father's routine as King was to change the time for the weekly audience with the prime minister from 5.30pm to 6.30pm. This allowed her to join her children in the nursery for their nightly bath and bedtime.

Thus began a lifetime of combining service to her country with her role as a parent, every bit of it under a scrutinising, often critical public eye. Like any mother, she has had her share of missteps, dramas and rifts with her children. Like all children, they have turned out not quite as she might have expected or planned.

Yet if one moment sums up Elizabeth's legacy as a mother and the reciprocal love of her children, it was during the Diamond Jubilee concert in 2012, when Charles addressed her in front of 18,000 people on a grandstand outside Buckingham Palace, and a further half a million watching on large screens in St James's Park, The Mall and Hyde Park. "Your Majesty – Mummy," he said, drawing an unusually huge public smile from her, and great cheers from the crowd. Then he thanked her "for inspiring us with your selfless duty and service, and for making us proud to be British".

From the outset of her reign, Elizabeth felt it essential to demonstrate her gravitas to the older men (and they were all men) who advised her. As a career woman, she was an anomaly in her generation and in the British upper class, combining the roles of monarch, wife and mother without any ready role model. She waited ten years before having her third child, Prince Andrew, and four years later Prince Edward was born, in 1964.

"Nothing, but nothing, deflected her from duty," recalled Sir Edward Ford, an assistant private secretary to the Queen. "She'd go into labour and have a baby, so we knew we weren't going to see her for a while.

The new Queen, Princess Anne and Prince Charles at Balmoral in 1952.

In the grounds of the palace with Prince Philip, Princess Anne and Prince Charles, 1957.

The Queen salutes with two-day-old Prince Edward in her arms and four-year-old Prince Andrew next to her on the palace balcony during Trooping the Colour in 1964.

Prince Philip, Prince Edward, the Queen, Prince Andrew, Princess Anne and Prince Charles in the grounds of Frogmore, on the Windsor estate, in 1968.

But within a very short time, 24 or 48 hours at most, she'd be asking whether there were any papers and would we care to send them up?" She took overseas trips as well; her first extensive tour of Commonwealth countries in 1953 and 1954 kept her away from Charles and Anne for nearly six months.

Her children were fortunate to have a nurturing nanny in Mabel Anderson, who was only a year younger than the Queen and had an affectionate and flexible nature as well as a firm sense of right and wrong. Their maternal grandmother, the Queen Mother, was also an important force who particularly doted on Prince Charles – sometimes to the point of cosseting.

Clarissa Eden, the wife of the then prime minister Anthony Eden (later the 1st Earl of Avon), was perplexed that the Queen and the Queen Mother failed to discipline six-year-old Charles during a picnic at Windsor Castle when he refused to yield his chair to the prime minister. Lady Avon was surprised that the Queen "didn't say, 'Come on, Charles, get up,' but I suppose she doesn't like scenes at all costs".

All her children knew that she spent long hours in her office at Buckingham Palace, where her priorities were, as Prince Andrew put it, "work and responsibilities and duties". While the Queen certainly loved her children, she fell into professional habits that pulled her away from motherhood. As a result, she missed out on many maternal challenges as well as pleasures. "She let things go," said Gay Charteris, the wife of the Queen's long-time private secretary Martin Charteris. "She did have work every day. It was easier to go back to that than children having tantrums. She always had the excuse of the red boxes." "She was not a hugger," agreed the Queen's first cousin, Lady Mary Clayton. "She has a different nature. There is a self-containment."

The Queen was more visibly engaged with her second set of children. When Mabel Anderson took time off, the Queen felt relaxed enough to stay in the nursery with Andrew and Edward, tying on an apron for their baths and lulling them to sleep.

During weekends at Windsor Castle, the boys zoomed down the gilded Grand Corridor in their pedal cars, and if they fell off their bicycles on one of the gravel paths in the park, the Queen would "pick them up and say, 'Don't be so silly. There's nothing wrong with you. Go and wash off' just like any parent," Prince Andrew recalled. At teatime, she joined them to watch the BBC's *Grandstand* sports programme on Saturdays and the Sunday cricket league.

All four children found common ground with both parents during their holidays at the family's rural estates, Sandringham in Norfolk and Balmoral in Aberdeenshire. The Queen and Prince Philip taught their children to appreciate their natural surroundings and instructed them how to shoot as well as how to cast into the pools of the River Dee and catch salmon with a well-tied fly. They stalked stag with their parents at Balmoral, and they spent hours on horseback across what Anne remembered as the "miles of stubble fields around Sandringham" and among "the autumn colours of the rowans and silver birches, the majesties of the old Scots pines" at Balmoral.

It was perhaps here, away from the pressures of duty, that the Queen was able to bond best with her children, and where she was most able to be herself. In more recent decades, the Queen has cultivated a love of country pursuits in her grandchildren too. By the time they were teenagers, Prince William and Prince Harry were regulars on the Scottish grouse moors and at Sandringham for pheasant shoots. Edward, the Earl of Wessex, is a keen shot and attends shoots at Sandringham with his son James, Viscount Severn, now himself in his teens.

The press of her duties prompted the Queen to make her husband the ultimate arbiter in decisions about their children. She believed Prince Philip's role as head of the family was "the natural state of things". He enforced discipline, and he selected their children's schools, which in the case of Charles reflected Philip's belief in the merit of his own experience rather than what was appropriate for his diffident, sensitive and awkward eldest son.

Charles hated Gordonstoun, the boarding school in Scotland that he found severe, although his younger brothers fared better, not least because by then the atmosphere was more humane with the inclusion of girls. Princess Anne, whose self-confidence and assertiveness mirrored her father's personality, did well at Benenden, her boarding school in Kent.

Particularly with her two eldest children, Charles and Anne, the Queen believed in the necessity of exposing them to challenging situations and talking to them "on level grown-up terms". "I remember the patience Prince Charles showed when he was around all those adults,'" said Mary Wilson, the wife of the Labour prime minister Harold Wilson. The royal children may have grown up in a bubble, but the Queen wanted them to work through difficulties and learn to think for themselves. "I learnt the way a monkey learns – by watching its parents," Charles once said.

During Anne's trip to New Zealand with her parents in 1970, the "walkabout" was introduced into the royal routine, a casual stroll to chat and shake hands with ordinary people. "At 19 years old, suddenly being dropped in the middle of the street," Anne recalled. "Suddenly being told to pick someone and talk to them. Fun? No, I don't think so."

Anne had a strong bond with her mother through horses, especially when she became a top competitor in the arduous equestrian sport of three-day eventing. She was married at a young age, in 1973, to Captain Mark Phillips, an accomplished horseman who won an Olympic gold medal.

The Queen's laissez-faire attitude led to unfortunate consequences when her children reached adulthood, giving her more than her share of heartache. The Countess of Leicester, a neighbour in Norfolk and one of the Queen's ladies-in-waiting, recalled a time when they were writing letters together under an awning at Sandringham.

"Suddenly from the bushes to the left there were screams and giggles," the countess later told her daughter, Lady Glenconner. "Around the corner came Andrew dragging the gardener's daughter, her dress in disarray. The Queen took no notice and kept on dictating the letters."

Andrew distinguished himself as a helicopter pilot who saw combat during the Falklands conflict in 1982. On his return after more than five months away, the Queen appeared to wipe tears from her eyes during the flag-waving homecoming at Portsmouth, as her second son greeted her with a red rose between his teeth. She was genuinely pleased in 1986 when he married Sarah Ferguson, a robust and jolly young woman who shared the monarch's love of riding and other country pursuits.

Edward, who had his mother's shy streak, struggled after earning his degree at Cambridge. He first bailed out of training as a Royal Marine and then stumbled in trying to establish himself as a film producer. He finally found his footing when he teamed up with his father in running the Duke of Edinburgh's awards for young people. Edward's much later marriage, at the age of 35, to Sophie Rhys-Jones, a middle-class public relations consultant, drew him closer to his mother.

"Sophie first of all respects her as the Queen, then as a mother-in-law, but she also understands that she is a human being and treats her that way," observed the Queen's cousin, Lady Elizabeth Anson.

Throughout his life, the Queen has "allowed Prince Charles to work at his interests, his aims and his ambitions" said Sir Malcolm Ross, one of her senior advisers. "It is not a cosy relationship," said the Queen's cousin Margaret Rhodes. "They love each other, but the family is not set up to be cosy."

The absence of cosiness made her children's marital break-ups much more difficult for the Queen to recognise and understand, especially with Charles and Diana, Princess of Wales. "I think it took a long time to accept that the faults were not more his than hers," said Patricia Mountbatten, her third cousin. In 1992 – what the Queen called her "annus horribilis" when Anne, Charles and Andrew split from their spouses – she found it all "nonplussing", recalled Mountbatten. "You don't know how to behave when someone is making such a mess. You want to help them mend, but how to do it?"

The publication in 1994 of Prince Charles's officially sanctioned biography drove a wedge between the heir and his parents. The author Jonathan Dimbleby quoted his complaints that the Queen had been remote during his unhappy childhood and that Philip had been overbearing and insensitive. His parents were wounded and his three siblings were indignant and rebuked Charles to his face.

A decade later, after another book that elaborated on these themes, Princess Anne countered that "it just beggars belief" to suggest that her mother was aloof and uncaring, adding that she and her brothers "understood what the limitations were in time and the responsibilities placed on her". Anne said they all appreciated being "allowed to find our own way ... People have to make their own mistakes. I think she's always accepted that."

The Queen has steered the monarchy steadily across the decades, reinforcing its place as the linchpin of the country's identity even as she moved subtly with the times. More fundamentally, however, she presides over a modern and effective royal family, despite the hiccups along the way.

As in any family, these will always occur, the most significant of recent times being the rift with the Sussexes – Harry and Meghan – and the fall-out from Andrew's association with Jeffrey Epstein, the abuser of young women, which in 2019 led to the Duke of York retreating from his public duties.

Yet otherwise, after decades of turbulence, her children have settled down, found happiness and worked hard to earn the admiration and affection of the people. With their visible commitment to public service and fulfilment of their royal duties, it is clear that their mother trained them well, instilling in them the values and traditions essential to the institution she still so brilliantly leads.

Driving in Windsor in 1957, with Prince Charles and Princess Anne
in the passenger seats to the delight of onlookers.

With Prince Charles, Prince Edward and Prince Andrew at the Montreal Olympics, July 1976.

At the 1968 Eridge Horse Trials in East Sussex, where Princess Anne was competing.

Explaining the finer points of Trooping the Colour to Prince Edward at Buckingham Palace, c 1972.

THE QUEEN AND DIANA
by Valentine Low

In one of the most memorable, if not exactly subtle, scenes in the 2006 film *The Queen*, after the death of Diana, Princess of Wales, Helen Mirren comes face to face with a magnificent lone deer that, after a long stare, she shoos away in an attempt to save its life.

Whether this captured the Queen's view of Diana is questionable; after all, it was in fact Diana's brother, Charles Spencer, who called her the most hunted person of the modern age. While sympathetic, the Queen also thought her daughter-in-law behaved badly; she never understood her.

It has always been her attitude not to try to cause trouble, a tendency that showed itself when Prince Charles was considering marrying Diana. While the Queen Mother was strongly in favour, the Queen, according to Charles's biographer Jonathan Dimbleby, "characteristically ... refrained from tendering her opinion".

While Charles and the palace machine never really knew what to do with Diana, the Queen was never less than supportive. The problem, perhaps, was that she was never anything more than supportive either. Diana revered the Queen but the aura that surrounded her, together with the Queen's natural reserve, meant that they never achieved anything like intimacy.

As early as her honeymoon, Diana had the capacity to leave the Queen baffled. At Balmoral, when she had a fit of sulks and refused to come down to dinner, the Queen was mystified as to how someone could behave so badly.

While the Queen is said to have liked the glamour Diana brought to the monarchy, it gave her daughter-in-law a power she quickly learnt to use. As relations with Charles went from bad to worse the Queen found herself increasingly torn over how to react.

The Princess of Wales and the Queen at the state opening of parliament in 1982.

The Queen preferred not to intervene in Charles and Diana's troubled marriage.

Diana recounted how whenever the subject of her marriage came up, the Queen would look worried and twiddle her glasses in her hands. Later, according to her lover James Hewitt, Diana summoned up the courage to have a frank discussion with her mother-in-law about her problems. "The Queen promised she would do what she could to take some pressure off her, and newspaper editors were asked not to subject her to too much scrutiny," said Hewitt. "But when it came to the issue of her marriage to Charles, the Queen said there was nothing she could do. It would be wrong to intervene."

The Queen did her best to remain neutral: whatever Diana had done, she and Philip also disapproved of Charles's own infidelity with Camilla Parker Bowles (as she was). However, when the Queen wrote to say that divorce was in the country's best interests, Diana was furious.

The Queen's failure to understand Diana became, after her death in a car accident in Paris in 1997, a failure to understand the nation's grief. She stayed in Balmoral, thinking it was best for her grandsons; the people thought otherwise. Nearly a week later, she briefly appeared in The Mall to look at flowers and later addressed the country.

Speaking "as your Queen and as a grandmother", she called Diana "an exceptional and gifted human being" and said there were "lessons to be drawn from her life and from the extraordinary and moving reaction to her death".

The Duke of Edinburgh and the Queen survey the floral tributes to Diana on The Mall.

A NEW
ELIZABETHAN AGE

A TRUE ANNUS HORRIBILIS

by Valentine Low

On November 24, 1992, the Queen had a heavy cold. It had been exacerbated by the smoke from the fire that devastated Windsor Castle and it gave added poignancy to a speech she made at Guildhall marking her 40 years on the throne.

"Nineteen ninety-two is not a year on which I shall look back with undiluted pleasure," she said. "In the words of one of my more sympathetic correspondents, it has turned out to be an annus horribilis."

It had, indeed, been a terrible year for the royal family: as well as the fire, the marriages of the Queen's three eldest children were all in the process of collapse. Perhaps more importantly the speech marked a turning point in the royal family's relationship with the British people. Bleak in both content and delivery, with its talk of how no institution could expect to be free from scrutiny, the speech was either an appeal for forbearance and understanding or an act of penitence.

It was also a heavy hint of what was to come only two days later. In the Commons, John Major, the prime minister, announced that the following year the Queen and the Prince of Wales would start paying tax on their private income, and that £900,000 of Civil List payments to other members of the royal family would come to an end.

Of the three marriage breakdowns, at least the Queen knew one was coming: the divorce of Princess Anne and Mark Phillips, who had been separated for some years, was finalised in April. The tabloids were rarely short of tittle-tattle from the other two. In January, photographs were published of the Duchess of York on holiday with her Texan friend Steve Wyatt. Six days later the duke and duchess decided to separate.

The Prince and Princess of Wales, meanwhile, were conducting a highly public marital war. However, nothing prepared people for the shock of the serialisation in *The Sunday Times* in June of Andrew Morton's book *Diana: Her True Story*.

Readers learnt how Diana had deliberately thrown herself down the stairs at Sandringham, and had even slashed her wrists with a razor blade. Her bulimia and depression were charted in devastating detail. While Diana was portrayed as vulnerable and unable to cope, Charles was castigated for his lack of understanding and his relationship with Camilla Parker Bowles.

The Queen was both furious and deeply troubled by it all. In her biography of the Queen, Sarah Bradford painted a vivid picture of the awkward atmosphere at Royal Ascot that year, with Prince Philip refusing to talk to Diana and the Queen in "a pretty bad temper", according to one of her guests.

The scandals kept on coming. In August, the *Daily Mirror* published a picture of the Duchess of York topless by a pool as her friend and so-called financial adviser, John Bryan, kissed her toes. *The Sun* published the transcript of a telephone conversation between Diana and James Gilbey, in which he called her "Squidgy" and she described her marriage as "torture". Another recording surfaced in November, courtesy of *The Sun*. This time it was the Prince of Wales and Camilla Parker Bowles, and featured the prince uttering such toe-curling endearments as "Your great achievement is to love me."

Discontent about the royals' tax affairs rumbled on. Behind the scenes, moves were already afoot to address the tax question. In public, however, it looked as if the royal family was on the back foot, with both Labour and Tory MPs calling for reform.

Then, on November 20, fire broke out at Windsor Castle after a restorer's lamp set a curtain alight. St George's Hall suffered extensive damage, along with the state dining room and three drawing rooms. Although there was sympathy for the royals, in a woeful misreading of the public mood, the heritage secretary Peter Brooke announced that as the castle was uninsured, the government would foot the repair bill, estimated at £20 million–£40 million. The restoration was later paid for without any recourse to public funds.

On December 9 came the announcement of the separation of the Prince and Princess of Wales. Days later, *The Sun* published the text of the Queen's Christmas broadcast before it went out. The Queen successfully sued for breach of copyright. It would take time, however, before the royal family's standing recovered.

Fire swept through Windsor Castle in November 1992.

Prince Andrew said the Queen was "shocked and devastated" by the damage caused to Windsor Castle.

The Queen Shares Her Sadness

The Queen returned to London to face her people yesterday, and they left her in no doubt that she was welcome.

At two public appearances she looked at times red-eyed and only just within the bounds of composure, at times astonished at the mountains of flowers and the size of the crowds and, in brief flashes of smile, relieved that any mild criticism of the Crown displaying insufficient public mourning seemed to have been forgiven by her presence.

As the Queen and the Duke of Edinburgh arrived from Balmoral at the Buckingham Palace gates, they got out of the car to look at the flowers and tributes to her late former daughter-in-law draped along the entire frontage. Turning to her husband, she shook her head as she pointed to the carpet of floral tributes. She saw too a poignant reminder of recent disquiet: a small Union Flag at half-mast left by one of the many thousands who had come to grieve.

Slowly the Queen walked along the lines of flowers, occasionally leaning down to read a message, pointing out a child's toy or a memorable photograph to Prince Philip.

She looked moved by the unforeseen and unprecedented expression of public grief. For several moments the royal couple stood together, heads bowed, lost in thought at the thousands of handwritten tributes, many of which were critical of their monarch.

As the crowd realised the Queen was walking among the flowers, they broke into applause. She turned for a second, smiled then returned to gaze on the endless succession of simple tributes. She told one woman: "I never realised there had been so many flowers left; it is remarkable."

Dressed in black with a simple hat and three strings of pearls, the Queen spent ten minutes walking back and forth before the crowd, with bouquets pressed into her hands and those of the Duke at almost every step.

Before she retired back into the palace she turned to look down The Mall, by now a sea of faces almost as far as she could see. However much her advisers had briefed her on the events and the mood in London, she was patently unprepared for the sheer size of the public expressions of sympathy for the Princess.

The story was the same at St. James's Palace, where the Queen and the Duke spent 15 minutes privately in the Chapel Royal, where the body of the Princess lies before the altar under Holbein's painted ceiling commemorating Henry VIII's brief marriage to Anne of Cleves. As she emerged from the palace, a waiting crowd of thousands broke into applause. Briefly, the Queen smiled, and went straight to another spontaneous display of flowers on the pavement. She made for the head of the queue, still hundreds of yards long, that for five days has shuffled towards the books of condolence.

Fred Cultworthy, 44, pressed a single rose in her hand. "I bought it for Diana, but I gave it to the Queen so that she would not think everybody thought the same way as some newspapers," he said.

Laura Trant, 15, said: "We told her how sorry we were, and we told her to look after the boys. She said 'I will'. She couldn't believe how hard it was for them because they were so young. Her mouth was quivering and her eyes were tearful."

As the Queen walked the first hundred yards of the queue, many others expressed their feelings about the young princes. She told one woman: "The boys are the important thing."

Beryl Holliday, 54, was glad to have spoken to the Queen. "Everybody here thinks it was worth the wait. I hope she has listened to the people."

The Times, September 6, 1997

Princess Diana's family watch the hearse depart at her funeral on September 6, 1997.

REINVENTING THE MONARCHY

by Damian Whitworth

The moment during her reign when the Queen's ability to reinvent the monarchy for the modern age was demonstrated most cleverly came when she starred as a Bond girl. Her agreement to participate in the opening ceremony of the 2012 Olympic Games with Daniel Craig was a master stroke. As she and 007 appeared to parachute into the stadium, the audience let out a gasp audible to the ceremony's television audience of 900 million. The six-minute film, showing the Queen and Craig in the grandeur of Buckingham Palace, then their stunt doubles throwing themselves out of a helicopter above the stadium, was a fusion of ancient royal mystique with modern wit.

The Queen's reign has spanned the TV age but she would not have considered anything so bold even a few years earlier. That she could provide the biggest surprise on a night of theatrical wonders was testimony to how shrewdly she had led the steady rebranding of "The Firm" after years when the share price had been heavily depressed.

In 2012, her Diamond Jubilee year, the Queen's approval ratings reached new heights. Ninety per cent of Britons said they were satisfied with how she did her job. Only 7 per cent said they were dissatisfied – the sort of figures of which elected heads of state can only dream. This marked a significant upturn in her popularity from the tumultuous 1990s when the monarchy reeled from one crisis to another, the public began to take a dim view and there was a rise in republican sentiment.

From those dark days the Queen has spearheaded a remarkable comeback in the fortunes of her family, showing the monarchy's ability to evolve, and securing its place in the future of these islands. As *The Times* put it during the Diamond Jubilee: "It is easy to forget, in the summer of 2012, that half a generation ago the royal house of Windsor had stretched the people's patience close to breaking point."

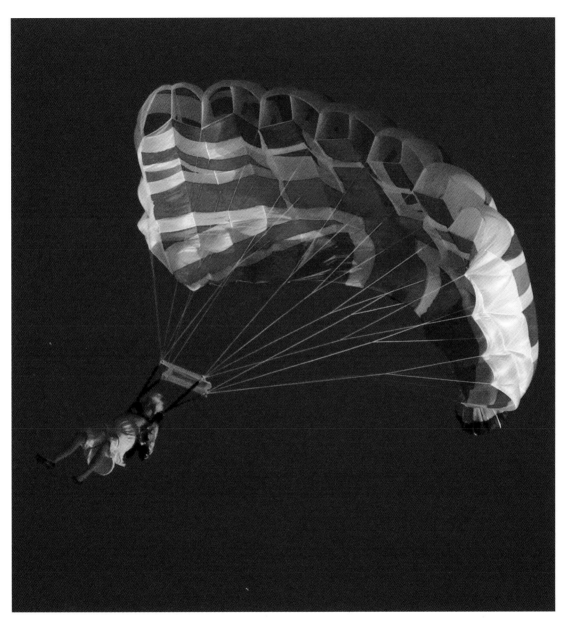

The Queen's stunt double parachutes into the Olympic Stadium.

The Queen formally opens the London Olympics on July 27, 2012.

An event by a republican pressure group attracted only 60 people, and chants of "Lizzie, Lizzie, Lizzie, Out, Out, Out" were drowned out by "God Save the Queen".

Sir David Attenborough, who was born a couple of weeks after the Queen, has joked that people often acquire "national treasure" status because they have been around such a long time. It is true that the Queen's longevity has contributed to her appeal. She has been on the throne throughout the lives of the majority of her subjects and as the years have elapsed between past tawdry events and the most recent images of her indefatigable dutifulness, there is a growing appreciation of her as a comforting presence. Through financial meltdown and political crisis, she has remained constant, calm and rarely emotional – unless one of her horses is winning. She has ploughed on with public appearances, private audiences and official briefings.

It is easier for a nation to feel well disposed towards a happy family, and as time has passed this one has looked so much happier. Camilla Parker Bowles, once so unpopular that she was pelted with rolls in a supermarket, has not only been brought into the fold but has been able to marry the heir to the throne and win public acceptance. More than that: with her down-to-earth humour and light touch, the Duchess of Cornwall proves popular when she accompanies the prince and helps him appear contented and relaxed.

The Duke of Cambridge went a step farther and married into the middle class. Kate Middleton's parents, former British Airways employees, run a mail-order party business and she has ancestors who were Geordie coalminers. Her wedding in 2011 to Prince William saw a million people on the streets of London and hundreds of millions watching worldwide. It was a feelgood event at a time when the country had been mired in the longest period of austerity in living memory.

The Queen looks out from a carriage window at Edinburgh's Waverley Station, after boarding a steam train to inaugurate the £294 million Scottish Borders Railway, on September 9, 2015 – the day she became Britain's longest-reigning monarch.

A packed Mall during the Queen's Diamond Jubilee on June 5, 2012.

Prince Philip, the Queen, the Duchess of Cornwall and the Duchess of Cambridge on board the Spirit of Chartwell *on a very wet day at the Diamond Jubilee pageant on the Thames.*

*The Duchess of Cambridge and the Queen watch a children's sports
event in Nottingham during the Diamond Jubilee year.*

George, Charlotte and Louis have completed the picture of a fully functional family that has rediscovered its mojo and is closer to the rest of the population than before. George, born to live in a palace, spends many weekends with his mother's parents who have proved hands-on grandparents in a way that a future king has probably never experienced before.

The maturing of Prince Harry during his late twenties, when he showed humour and much of his mother's humanity on tours and in charity work, helped him to become a popular member of the clan. His own step farther, his marriage in 2018 to a mixed-race, and divorced, American actress, Meghan Markle, similarly had the effect of refreshing the brand, even if the new gilt was tarnished by the Sussexes' move to California and the subsequent public rift with the family. Its impact on the future of the monarchy itself, however, is likely to be limited.

The royal family plots its long-term strategy carefully and has benefited in recent decades from the professionalisation of its household. Though the family is traditionally comfortable surrounded by aristocrats, the Queen's key advisers during the years of transformation were her private secretary, Sir Christopher (now Lord) Geidt, and his predecessor Lord Janvrin, both former diplomats.

The household has embraced social media but has not lost its ability to pull off the best pageantry in the world. There were the two royal weddings and, in 2012, the Diamond Jubilee weekend. This extravaganza concluded with a service at St Paul's Cathedral and a balcony appearance at the palace that featured only six family members: the Queen, the Prince of Wales, the Duchess of Cornwall, the Duke and Duchess of Cambridge and Prince Harry. The tableau sent a message that here was a streamlined unit focused on keeping the family business going.

Earlier a 1,000-strong flotilla processed down the Thames on a miserably wet day when onlookers and monarch were united in a soggy, dogged desire to celebrate the glorious nuttiness of being British. At the celebratory concert Madness sang "Our house, in the middle of one's street" from the roof of Buckingham Palace. Britain felt like one nation.

When the Queen became the UK's longest-reigning monarch she was less keen to celebrate. The moment arrived on the afternoon of Wednesday, September 9, 2015, when she had been on the throne for 23,226 days, 16 hours and 23 minutes, passing Queen Victoria's record. For various reasons, not least that her accession was bound up with the death of her father, she was reluctant to make any fuss, but eventually agreed to open the Scottish Borders Railway that day.

Standing next to Scotland's first minister, Nicola Sturgeon, after journeying by steam train from Edinburgh to Tweedbank, the Queen alluded briefly to her new place in the history books. "Many, including you, first minister, have also kindly noted another significance attaching to today, although it is not one to which I have ever aspired. Inevitably, a long life can pass by many milestones; my own is no exception. But I thank you all, and the many others at home and overseas, for your touching messages of great kindness."

Prince William chauffeurs his bride from the palace after their wedding reception on April 29, 2011.

Left: Prince Charles and the Duchess of Cornwall take part, with gusto, in a parachute game at a youth festival in Guernsey, July 2012. Right: The RAF's Red Arrows execute a flypast for the Diamond Jubilee.

Prince George accompanied his parents, the Duke and Duchess of Cambridge, on a trip to Canada in 2016.

JUST GRANNY

by Damian Whitworth

To the world she is the Queen, but to her eight grandchildren she is "Granny". The Duke of Cambridge once explained the reality of growing up as a grandson of the most famous woman in the world. "She's my grandmother to me first and then she's the Queen."

This was demonstrated most clearly in the hours after the death of his mother, Diana, Princess of Wales, in 1997. The Queen was widely criticised when she did not return from Balmoral to London where large crowds were mourning. On this occasion, however, her instincts as a grandmother trumped her sense of duty as Queen. Her first priority was to stay with William and Harry in Scotland and help them grieve in private.

Long before then William had developed a close bond with his grandmother, whose weekend home was a short walk from his school. Most weekends during his years at Eton he would walk across the river to spend time at Windsor Castle with "Granny". He and Harry both shouted, "Go, Granny!" during the opening ceremony of the 2012 Olympics when a stunt appeared to show Her Majesty parachuting out of a helicopter with Daniel Craig's James Bond.

After his wedding in 2011, Prince William offered a fascinating insight into how the Queen could cut through royal pomp to ensure he and his intended bride were not swamped by tradition. Once William had announced his engagement to Kate Middleton, palace bureaucracy swung into action on a scale that alarmed the prince.

"I was given this official list of 777 names – dignitaries, governors, all sorts of people – and not one person I knew," he recalled. "They said: 'These are the people we should invite.' I looked at it in absolute horror and said: 'I think we should start again.'

"I rang [the Queen] up the next day and said: 'Do we need to be doing this?' And she said: 'No. Start with your friends first and then go from there.' And she told me to bin the list. She made the point that there are certain times when you have to strike the right balance. And it's advice like that which is really key, when you know that she's seen and done it before."

The Queen's grandchildren are Prince William and Prince Harry, sons of the Prince of Wales; Princess Beatrice and Princess Eugenie, the daughters of the Duke of York; Peter Phillips and Zara Tindall, the children of the Princess Royal; Lady Louise Windsor and James, Viscount Severn, the offspring of the Earl of Wessex.

She also has 11 great-grandchildren: Prince George, Princess Charlotte and Prince Louis; Archie and Lilibet Mountbatten-Windsor; Savannah and Isla Phillips; Mia, Lena and Lucas Tindall; and August Brooksbank, the son of Princess Eugenie. The Queen particularly enjoys her annual pre-Christmas lunch at Buckingham Palace, which provides an opportunity to get together as much of the extended family as possible.

The Queen is also known as "Granny" to Prince George. That became clear after Charlotte's christening, when William was heard telling him "we can go back to Granny's". That would be Sandringham, the main house on the estate where they also live, in Anmer Hall.

The Duke of York once suggested that the Queen had been more comfortable as a grandmother than she had been a mother, which was hardly surprising given that she was a young woman when she had to juggle motherhood with monarchy.

"She's been a fantastic grandmother to Beatrice and Eugenie and probably revels in that more than being a mother, to some extent. Always interested and concerned for what the girls are up to," Prince Andrew said at the time of her Diamond Jubilee.

The grandchildren...

Peter Phillips
(son of the
Princess Royal)

Zara Tindall
(daughter of the
Princess Royal)

Prince Harry
(son of the
Prince of Wales)

Prince William
(son of the
Prince of Wales)

Princess Eugenie
*(daughter of the
Duke of York)*

Princess Beatrice
*(daughter of the
Duke of York)*

Lady Louise Windsor
*(daughter of the
Earl of Wessex)*

James, Viscount Severn
*(son of the
Earl of Wessex)*

Eugenie describes a grandmother who "lights up" around her grandchildren. She would take them raspberry picking when she was young and listened to Eugenie's stories of life at Newcastle University, taking an interest in what essays she was writing.

In recent years the Queen has been very close to her youngest grandchildren, the children of the Earl of Wessex, who decided against giving them the titles of prince and princess. The family live at Bagshot Park, a short drive from Windsor, where the children often go riding with their grandmother.

As a young girl, Lady Louise, now in her late teens, bore a striking physical resemblance to her grandmother at the same age, and she spends time talking horses with the Queen at the Royal Mews at Windsor where her pony is stabled.

The Queen likes nothing more than to attend events where she has a role as both grandmother and Queen. At William's passing-out parade at Sandhurst in 2006 she managed to make her grandson smile as she inspected the solemn-faced new officers in her role as commander-in-chief of the armed forces. William said that his grandmother likes to laugh about things that have gone wrong at formal events. "The Queen has seen so many parades or performances, when there's a small slip-up it tickles her humour."

He also says, however, that for a grandson who will one day sit on the throne, she is a constant source of counsel. "There's no question you can ask, and no point you can raise, that she won't already know about – and have a better opinion about," he told the author Robert Hardman for his book *Our Queen*. "And for me particularly, being the young bloke coming through, being able to talk to my grandmother, ask her questions and know that there's sound advice coming back is very reassuring."

After going to see victims of the Australian floods and New Zealand earthquake in 2011 William received a note from the Queen congratulating him on the way he represented her. "When you get a letter from her or a bit of praise, it goes a long, long way, more so than anyone else saying, 'Well done' to you. There's such gravitas behind those words."

She has seen her grandchildren make mistakes, but their indiscretions come with the added complication that they were often splashed across newspapers: Harry in a Nazi uniform, smoking cannabis or playing strip poker in Las Vegas; William landing his helicopter in the back garden of Kate's parents' home.

One of the few occasions when Buckingham Palace made it clear that the monarch disapproved of a grandchild's behaviour was when Peter Phillips sold the photographs of his wedding at Windsor Castle to *Hello!* magazine. And there were raised eyebrows when his sister, Zara, and her husband, Mike Tindall, appeared in the same magazine with their daughter Mia.

There is no doubt that in private the Queen can be clear and forthright when she needs to be. William may have found Granny was relaxed about the wedding guest list but when he started weighing up which military uniform he would wear on the day, she told him there was no question he should wear his Irish Guards uniform. "I was given a categorical, 'No, you'll wear this.' So you don't always get what you want, put it that way."

Prince William can't help smiling at his grandmother during his passing-out parade at Sandhurst, 2006.

Harry with his grandmother after Prince Charles's wedding to Camilla Parker Bowles, 2005.

The Queen has always shared a passion for horses with her grandchildren, especially Zara Tindall, pictured here at the Cheltenham Gold Cup race meeting in March 2003.

The Queen with Princess Eugenie at the traditional Royal Maundy Service at St George's Chapel, 2019.

THE FUTURE:
GEORGE, CHARLOTTE & LOUIS

by Valentine Low

It is a close call as to which has the greater power to increase the popularity of the monarchy: a royal wedding or a royal birth. However, there was no doubt that the arrival of Prince George in 2013 was yet another boost for the royal family's public standing. Even the most curmudgeonly republicans silenced their complaints for a day.

Prince George was more than just a bonny baby, however. His birth heralded something far more important: it signified lineage and longevity. The point was brought home in fairly unsubtle style at George's christening in October of that year when an official photograph was released showing, for the first time since 1894, four generations of the royal family gathered together: the Queen, the Prince of Wales, the Duke of Cambridge and Prince George. The line of succession was, barring some terrible misfortune, safe for many decades to come.

The Queen, of course, was delighted at the birth of the third in line to the throne (her third great-grandchild). Two days after George was born, she took the rare step of driving to Kensington Palace to meet the new addition. Usually, visitors come to see her.

Prince George was an immediate international superstar. He was inundated with presents from all over the world, and he accompanied his parents to Australia and New Zealand the following year. At home, he has been a regular visitor to Buckingham Palace, where the duchess started taking him for weekly swimming lessons before he turned one – a habit that will have strengthened his relationship with his great-grandmother. He even went there on his first birthday, the same day that the Queen made a point of attending his birthday party at Kensington Palace.

As the third in line to the throne, Prince George immediately became an international superstar.

If the birth of Princess Charlotte in 2015 – in and out of the Lindo Wing at St Mary's Hospital in a day – was surrounded by marginally less excitement, as the line of succession had been secured, there was still plenty of fanfare, from gun salutes to the equally traditional vigil outside the hospital by foreign news crews.

By then, the Cambridges had moved into Anmer Hall on the Sandringham Estate, which can only have pleased the Queen, allowing her the opportunity to see George and Charlotte more frequently, and with far less public scrutiny, than she does in London. The arrival of Prince Louis of Cambridge in 2018 completed the family, even as the duke and duchess began to take on a larger and more prominent share of royal duties.

Then within a few years, Prince George started to be seen with his parents as they performed those duties, for instance attending the final of the European football championship at Wembley in 2021. The result, as England lost to Italy, no doubt disappointed him – although he may have to get used to that – but for the monarchy his identification with the nation's hopes was another milestone reached. The cycle had begun anew, and the future secured once more.

Left: The birth of Princess Charlotte on May 2, 2015.
Right: The birth of Prince Louis on April 23, 2018.

The Duke and Duchess of Cambridge with their three children,
George, Charlotte and Louis, at the Trooping the Colour ceremony, 2019.

~ A Prince's Repose ~

A Christian funeral is a ceremony to honour the departed and seek solace for their soul. It also has a wider significance: to honour the person interred, recall their achievements in life and bring together in comfort and reverence those to whom he or she was closest. All these elements will mark the funeral today in St George's Chapel, Windsor, of the Duke of Edinburgh. It will not be a state funeral, partly because of his own wish and partly because of the restrictions imposed by the coronavirus. But it will still be the most poignant event for the Queen in her long reign. It will bring to an end a royal partnership that has brought stability and continuity to the United Kingdom for almost all the postwar era. And it heralds the transition to a new concept of monarchy that will, in future, be very different from what Prince Philip knew.

The symbolism of today's events has been planned in meticulous detail. Those attending, limited to no more than 30 in accordance with current restrictions affecting every funeral in the country, have been invited because of warm family ties and because of their personal friendship with the prince. Neither the prime minister nor any other political dignitary will be present. Civic leaders have already expressed, often eloquently, the nation's debt to Prince Philip over the past week of official mourning. It has been a difficult decision for the Queen to choose which duke, princess, cousin and grandchild to include and which will have to watch the ceremonies, like millions of Britons and people around the world, on television. But three of the mourners are of particular significance: the princes from Germany who are part of Prince Philip's extended family there and elsewhere in continental Europe.

Although himself a distant descendant of Queen Victoria, Prince Philip was not a native Briton. He adopted this country, and on his marriage dedicated his life to serving it as wholeheartedly as he had served during the war in the Royal Navy. None of his older sisters, married to Germans, was invited to his wedding: in 1947 popular sentiment was still raw. But the prince, whose early schooling was in Germany and who remained close to his German relatives throughout his life, brought a wider international perspective to the monarchy. He travelled to almost every country in the world, and with the Queen was a vigorous champion of the Commonwealth. His death has been mourned there to a degree that many younger Britons may not have realised: in Canada, Australia and New Zealand, and also in the Caribbean, the south Pacific and remote British overseas territories, he was seen as a figure who knew and understood their peoples even if official London seemed increasingly distant.

Much has been made of the naval and military symbols and personnel who will escort the coffin to the chapel, together with the choice of the "Eternal Father" hymn invoking those at sea (though not to be sung by the congregation, in keeping, again, with restrictions). The navy was where Prince Philip's heart lay. The Land Rover that he himself designed to bear his coffin represents his own intense interest in engineering and technology. More surprising, perhaps, is the decision that military uniforms are not to be worn. This partly reflects the prince's wish for a pared-down ceremony without flamboyance or fuss. It is also an appropriate way to avoid embarrassing Prince Harry, who is no longer entitled to wear a uniform.

The public will naturally look for signs of any reconciliation between Prince Harry and his elder brother, the Duke of Cambridge, after the frosty public comments made about him in Prince Harry's television interview. In walking behind the coffin, the brothers will be diplomatically separated by their cousin, Peter Phillips.

The issue is symbolic now of the challenge facing not only the Queen but increasingly the Prince of Wales, who will inevitably take over more of the monarch's official duties. Questions abound. How should the monarchy adapt to new times and changed expectations? To what extent do the foibles and antics of the wider royal family damage the monarchy's purpose? Would a more narrow focus allow younger princes and princesses to escape the attention and also the censure they have incurred? Indeed, should they have titles at all if not close to the throne?

As Prince Charles has clearly understood, and as shown by the number of complaints the BBC received over what was seen as excessive coverage, a younger generation no longer has the same interest in the royal family or deference to its constitutional role. Prince Philip, in his younger days, was central to efforts to modernise royal protocol, define royal duties, cut free from the flummery that seemed to envelop the institution, and keep the monarchy in tune with contemporary social attitudes. His achievement, in the face of much opposition, was significant and accounts largely for the monarchy's enduring popularity.

But times and views have changed. It is only 19 years since there was an outpouring of popular emotion and ceremonial pomp that marked the funeral of the Queen Mother. Those emotions have given way sometimes to indifference and occasionally to exasperation. Public comment on Prince Andrew has been personal and hostile; coverage of the monarchy has tended to focus now on cost and privilege. The foibles and rivalries that once entertained many Britons, and especially European tabloids, are seen as something more destructive that could tear apart a family once so united for its balcony appearances.

Prince Philip witnessed a long decline in the economic power, global influence and moral authority of the country he had made his own. He and the Queen have presided over the transformation of empire to

Commonwealth. More recently, there has been fierce public controversy over how the legacy of empire should be assessed. Britain, however, even when no longer joined with its former partners in the European Union, remains a country of immense achievement, promise and influence. And the monarchy remains central to the concept of nationhood, even if the unity of the United Kingdom may now be called into question. Those proposing its abolition have yet to offer an alternative that commands popular support and the backing of a long history and heritage.

The Duke of Edinburgh's death may seem to many to mark the closure of an age. In truth, it is part of an ever-changing institution that is defined as much by its principal players as by the expectations of those it serves. Prince Philip, for all the stories that have emerged of his contrariness and occasional hauteur, was a man of moral strength and humane vision. He led his family and influenced its actions in a way that even the Queen was happy to acknowledge and salute. He will be laid to rest today with the thanks of a nation for a life well lived and a purpose well served.

The Times, April 17, 2021

The Queen sits alone at Prince Philip's funeral, which took place on April 17, 2021, amid the restrictions set during the coronavirus pandemic.

Prince Philip, Duke of Edinburgh: June 10, 1921, to April 9, 2021.

AFTER PHILIP
by Matthew Dennison

At Buckingham Palace, scaffolding obscures the grand staircase. Largely out of action are the famous curving stairs, with their sweep of gilded balustrade, out of sight the soaring portraits of William IV and Queen Adelaide at the stairs' summit.

Typically, every year, the state apartments dazzle an admiring public. This year, much of the palace looks more like a building site; even rooms not subject to repairs have been repurposed as (admittedly grand) storage spaces. The programme of upgrading services throughout the palace – due for completion in time for the Platinum Jubilee – is not a glamorous one; wall pipes are being replaced and new water tanks installed; leaking roofs are being fixed, including re-roofing the picture gallery; a new energy centre is being built.

Even the royal family's private apartments, including the Queen's, are being licked into shape, a process made easier by the pandemic, which led to the Queen and her children vacating the capital's smartest office spaces to work from home in the country. In the Queen's case, this meant Windsor Castle. She retreated to Windsor in March 2020, to be shortly joined by Prince Philip, from his retirement home of Wood Farm on the Sandringham estate. There the couple lived with a reduced household of Covid-safe attendants affectionately labelled "HMS Bubble".

None of the Queen's ladies-in-waiting – that handful of women who accompany her on engagements and manage her correspondence, including, since 2017, two members of the Queen Mother's extended family, Susan Rhodes and Lady Elizabeth Leeming – was at the Queen's side continually throughout lockdown; the ladies-in-waiting also worked mostly from home. Now, offices in Buckingham Palace are returning to something approaching normality. Despite the scaffolding and disruption, insiders insist that it is still a working palace.

The message from palace staff is unequivocal: for Team Royal, it's business as usual. As always, the directive is the Queen's. At 95 and recently widowed, she remains the fountainhead. Her husband's death deprived her of the last of her closest family confidants, following the deaths of her sister, her mother and her cousin, Margaret Rhodes. But the Queen is not a sentimental woman. Her first mistress of the robes once described her as "very practical", and her sanctioning of wide-ranging palace repairs is also typical of her concern for the monarchy's future smooth running.

If it's business as usual for the palace, the same applies to its nonagenarian poster girl. Royal employees point out that the Queen's enjoyment of "getting out and about and meeting people" remains undimmed. One also reminds me of the promise of lifelong service she made in Cape Town in 1947. For the Queen, then, business as usual means going out and doing her duty, dressed in her customary bright colour-block outfits of coat and matching hat and with a smile on her face. As her former Archbishop of Canterbury Robert Runcie noted in the 1990s, "With her, duty comes first, even above family problems."

In the wake of the death of the Duke of Edinburgh, it has been an impressive show of resilience and dedication. At Windsor, in the final weeks of the duke's life, the couple's world shrank. Reunited by the pandemic, for a year they had been able to share the sort of leisurely togetherness other elderly couples enjoy, walking in the castle's private gardens and dining together without interruptions or the inevitable separations of busy public lives; they managed a last, short return to Wood Farm at the end of the summer.

After the duke's discharge from hospital, there was less time outside and formal meal times were abandoned. Philip slept a lot during the day, his appetite depleted, his mobility limited, although he continued to receive and write letters and stay in touch with close friends and family by telephone. The Queen understood the implications of his determination not to return to hospital. Although his death, on April 9, 2021, was peaceful and not unexpected, inevitably it shook the spouse who had fallen in love with her handsome, square-jawed prince at the age of 13. Prince Edward described his mother soon afterwards as "bearing up".

Whatever her unhappiness, it was almost certainly the Queen's wishes that restricted royal mourning for her beloved husband to two weeks, ending after his funeral, although the palace explained it at the time as a family decision. Nothing in her behaviour since has suggested a monarch hell-bent on protracted grieving in public. Perhaps she appeared unusually sombre at the state opening of parliament in May, the first ceremonial duty of her widowhood. Commentators who suggested the Queen had chosen to wear traditional half-mourning as a mark of her sadness overlooked her choice of the same flower-print frock she had previously worn on a happier occasion, for photographs released to mark Prince Philip's 99th birthday.

Nor did thoughts of Philip explain her absence from the first day of Royal Ascot. Instead, in her capacity as head of the Commonwealth and Queen of Australia, the Queen was at work, entertaining Australia's prime minister, Scott Morrison. She wore another brightly coloured frock and, in a characteristic diplomatic pleasantry, the large brooch of white and yellow diamonds, in the shape of Australia's national wattle flower, which Australians had presented to her on her first visit to the country in 1954. At the end of the week, she was present for the final day's racing at Ascot. Her decision to dispense with traditional black-bordered writing paper – instead, on the Queen's stationery, her crest appeared in black rather than red – also pointed to a desire to limit external signs of grief.

Indeed, some have observed how cheerful she has seemed when out and about. Perhaps this is to be expected after so many months of confinement; after all, at the time of the duke's death, many aspects of life had yet to open up. She was said to be spending her time in those early weeks tuning in to the BBC police drama *Line of Duty*, discussing the plot with one of her closest aides, Vice-Admiral Sir Tony Johnstone-Burt. There was additional sadness in May when a puppy given to her by the Duke of York died (she was reportedly given another on June 10, the centenary of Prince Philip's birth). Perhaps it's little wonder she appears so pleased to have resumed a busy schedule of public engagements.

For her return to full-time royal engagements the Queen gathered around her a small team of trusted intimates. As throughout lockdown, she remains in regular contact with members of her immediate family. Of her four children, Prince Andrew lives the closest, at Royal Lodge in Windsor Great Park, where the Queen spent much of her childhood. Eleven miles away are Prince Edward and his wife, Sophie, with whom the Queen shares a notably warm relationship, both unassuming, modest women and linked by interests including a fondness for military history.

In the Sussexes' absence, Princess Eugenie and her husband, Jack Brooksbank, have moved into Frogmore Cottage, giving the Queen a much-loved granddaughter within easy striking distance. In addition, the Queen has come to rely on the support of members of her household, including the lady-in-waiting who accompanied her to Prince Philip's funeral and Royal Ascot and her senior dresser. The first is 82-year-old Lady Susan Hussey, since 1996 Baroness Hussey, the second Angela Kelly.

In 2020 Hussey celebrated 60 years as a lady-in-waiting; her discretion, tact and humour have endeared her to generations of royals, including her godson, the Duke of Cambridge. In 2013 she received the Queen's highest mark of favour, when she was appointed Dame Grand Cross of the Royal Victorian Order, an honour more usually reserved for members of the Queen's family (other recipients include the Princess Royal, Princess Alexandra, the Countess of Wessex, the Duchess of Cornwall and the Duchess of Cambridge).

Kelly is a lively Liverpudlian divorcee in her early sixties and unashamedly devoted to the Queen. At intervals her meteoric career rise has inspired sniping within palace walls. Different in background, outlook and temperament, both women have earned and repaid the Queen's trust. Hussey shares a lifetime of memories with her royal employer, beginning with the birth of Prince Andrew. A widow since 2006, she can provide sympathetic companionable understanding.

The Queen surrounded herself with close aides after Prince Philip's death. She is pictured here with one of the closest, Vice-Admiral Sir Tony Johnstone-Burt.

After the Duke of Edinburgh's death, the Queen threw herself straight back into her royal duties,
here entertaining Australia's prime minister Scott Morrison.

Lady Hussey, lady-in-waiting, is a great support to the Queen.

The Queen has also come to rely on the support of Angela Kelly, her senior dresser.

That the Queen has chosen wisely is obvious to anyone who has witnessed recent engagements. At first, a view was widespread that the Duke of Edinburgh's death would inevitably lead to a scaling back in the Queen's public life as she grappled with her grief. There were even suggestions that, like Queen Victoria, she was planning to retreat to Balmoral and the privacy of the Highlands.

The Queen has indeed been in Scotland. Holyrood Week has long been a fixture in the royal diary and one the half-Scottish Queen looks forward to keenly. Usually she holds investitures and garden parties at her Edinburgh palace, but not in 2021, on account of Covid restrictions. Instead, the Queen went out and about. The Duke of Cambridge accompanied her on a visit to a soft drinks factory in Cumbernauld; two days later, with the Princess Royal, she visited a community nature reserve in Glasgow. In Edinburgh, again accompanied by her daughter, the Queen was given two young trees to be planted as part of a Platinum Jubilee conservation initiative, the Queen's Green Canopy. It was all a far cry from licking her wounds at Balmoral.

Like those of many of her subjects, the Queen's is a hybrid working life. Adept at Zoom, unlike her late husband, she has continued to carry out virtual engagements. New Ghanaian, Iranian, Israeli and Chinese ambassadors, for instance, were received virtually. The Queen spoke to leaders of the Queen's Commonwealth Trust, an initiative founded in her name in 2018 to raise funds for young people in the Commonwealth. For a sovereign in her tenth decade who no longer undertakes long-haul travel but remains head of a Commonwealth of 54 nations, the altered working practices of the pandemic offered an unexpected boon: the possibility of continuing her overseas work from home.

Although those in charge of the royal diary have been on standby for restart "for a while", the Queen's hybrid public life is likely to continue in this vein for some time. Resignedly – or perhaps it is simply a reflection of the Queen's unfussy pragmatism – everyone concerned appears quite happy with this. Plans are afoot for audiences with ambassadors to switch from virtual to physical; an in-person audience with the prime minister was widely publicised, but the Queen continues to deal with her governors-general virtually. Red boxes of state papers arrive at Windsor Castle daily; the business of state continues.

Undoubtedly, the Queen's life since Prince Philip's death has lacked the tranquillity of their final shared months. Although she was reported to have visited the Duke of Sussex after his arrival in the UK in July 2021 for the unveiling of a memorial to Diana, Princess of Wales, rifts within the royal family persist, described by Prince Edward as "difficult". There can be little doubt, however, that her return to public life, supported by her family and members of her inner circle, is a cause for pleasure for the elderly sovereign. The Queen told listeners to her Easter broadcast in 2020, "Dark as death can be … light and life are greater." All the evidence suggests she meant it.

The Queen's first trip to Scotland since the death of her husband.
Here, she visits Skypark in Glasgow on June 30, 2021, during Holyrood Week.

THE
LEGACY

A HARD ACT TO FOLLOW

by Ben Macintyre

One way to assess the legacy of Britain's longest-reigning monarch is to look back to where her story started. *The Times* of April 21, 1926, carried a very small announcement on page 14, between a report on ructions in the German cabinet and another on the progress of the economy bill: "The Duchess of York was safely delivered of a Princess at 2.40 this morning. Both mother and daughter are doing well." The baby would go on to become Elizabeth II.

Hers has been an extraordinary reign, not just for its longevity but for its strange and effective combination of consistency and adaptability, tradition and subtle innovation. She will leave the monarchy more secure than many would have predicted, but her very success leaves her heirs a problem: she will be a remarkably hard act to follow.

The newspaper on the day of her birth announcement reflected a secure, stratified society, a Britain that was still imperial and colonial; it was complacently and deeply royalist, confident in its collective identity. Reporting on the royal family was demure, discreet and, above all, deferential.

The Britain Elizabeth came to rule in 1952 was still recognisable as the one she had been born into. The news of her accession reached her in Kenya, then still firmly under British rule despite rumblings of rebellion. She had every reason to expect that she would rule in much the same way as her father and grandfather. It did not turn out that way.

As she observed in her Golden Jubilee speech of 2002: "Since 1952 I have witnessed the transformation of the international landscape ... matched by no less rapid developments at home, in the devolved shape of our nation, in the structure of society, in technology and communications, in our work and in the way we live."

The London of 1952 still had trams and smog. Churchill was still prime minister, and British troops were still fighting in Korea. The mathematician

Alan Turing was forced to undergo hormone treatment to avoid prison for his homosexuality. Britain remained an intensely traditional, old-fashioned realm with an enigma. She may have ruled for longer than any other British monarch, but few of her subjects can remember anything she has said. In the intrusive, fast-moving 20th century, she has proved that distance can be a source of royal strength.

So what does the legacy of Elizabeth II, and the way monarchy evolved under her, indicate about the coming reigns of Charles III, William V and, eventually, George VII? If the Elizabethan age is anything to go by (and it is), the monarchy of the future will be smaller, older, cannier, funnier, more reticent and micromanaged, underdressed in private moments and lavish in public ceremonial, more informal but not more intimate. Royalty will appear more middle class, while being nothing of the sort.

It will be run on business lines. Under Elizabeth, monarchy has just about broken even, but that has set up expectations of royal solvency; henceforth, it will have to show stakeholders a clear cultural profit.

The problems in Elizabeth's reign have come when modernity has collided with what the Victorian writer Walter Bagehot called the mystery and magic of "the charm of royalty". The family has suffered the sort of problems that afflict most other families: bereavement, failed marriages, younger members behaving badly. Yet whereas the deference of the first half of the century would have ensured such events were treated with decorum and euphemism, the insatiable curiosity of the second half of the 20th century and the start of the 21st meant that those moments have been scrutinised with brutal intensity.

As a consequence, the modern monarchy has become adept at presentational skills and the alchemy of public relations in a way that would have been unthinkable a generation ago. The key strategy (almost a mission statement) is now to enable the monarchy to appear more like the rest of us, while maintaining its mystery. The Duchess of Cambridge is the perfect embodiment of this approach, being university educated, well dressed, decorous, decorative and part of a middle-class family that appears almost quintessentially un-exotic and unthreatening. She has brilliantly absorbed the lessons of Elizabeth II's reign: smile, laugh even, put everyone at ease, say nothing controversial, and wear jeans as easily as a tiara.

There are now enough male royal heirs to last a century, and the future kings will have plenty of time to rehearse. To judge from the longevity of the Windsor bloodline, and based on actuarial calculations, William will be in his sixties before he wears the crown; George is likely to be even older.

When she succeeded her father, the 25-year-old Elizabeth was almost unknown to the British public. Even her nanny, Marion Crawford, who supposedly "told all" in 1950, told very little. Our future monarchs will be exceptionally well known to us by the time they succeed. What they do before becoming kings will matter just as much as what they do on the throne.

Older monarchs may have experience and maturity; the disadvantage is that with age come opinions. Queen Elizabeth has resolutely avoided intruding on politics; her son has shown no such self-restraint, insisting, in his own words, that he is "determined not to be confined to cutting ribbons". Perhaps the central question of the monarchy's future is the extent to which the institution can afford to become political. Too outspoken, and it risks fomenting division and controversy; too reticent, and it risks irrelevance.

Ever since the reign of Athelstan, who became the first king of all England in AD925, the British monarchy has survived by giving the impression that it remains a still point in a moving world, a bastion of tradition but adaptable with it. Elizabeth has maintained that illusion. Yet her successors will be required to be moving points in a world that is itself moving at staggering speed, transformed by global influences on British society, economic transition, social and ethnic migrations and radical institutional reform. Our national identity, so static and predictable at the time of Elizabeth's accession, is now in violent flux.

We are long past the time when monarchy could expect to be loved and revered simply for being, for the accident of breeding. It is a cliché to talk of a monarchy "winning" the respect of its people, but Elizabeth's reign has demonstrated just how easily even a popular queen can lose monarchy's popular purchase – and win it again. This is a judgmental, demanding and overachieving age.

The next generation of monarchs will have to do something more admirable than the run-of-the-mill royal activity: write something, explore something, prove something or achieve something. Some are born great, some have greatness thrust upon them; the next generation of royals will have to work harder for greatness than any before it.

Queen Elizabeth may come to be seen as the most successful monarch in British history, if success is measured by problems overcome, stability maintained and succession secured. She will leave a monarchy that is still recognisable, but also transformed, and certain to change yet more. Her subtle force of personality has kept the royal ship afloat; for her heirs, royal rule will also be a test of character and resolve.

Perhaps the most important aspect of Elizabeth's legacy will be the ethic of hard work, deep in old age. To live up to this shining example, her heirs will have to work their royal socks off.

The coronation of Elizabeth II at Westminster Abbey took place on June 2, 1953.

IMAGE CREDITS

pp.6–7: Max Mumby/Indigo
p.11: Max Mumby/Indigo
p.15: George Rinhart
p.18: Universal History Archive
p.19: Paul Popper/Popperfoto
p.22: Bob Thomas/Popperfoto
p.23: Bettmann
pp.24–25: Lisa Sheridan / Stringer
p.26: Paul Popper/Popperfoto
p.27: Lisa Sheridan / Stringer
p.29: Print Collector
p.31: Popperfoto
pp.32–33: Paul Popper/Popperfoto
p.34: Popperfoto
pp.36–37: Popperfoto
p.40: Bettmann
p.41: Lisa Sheridan / Stringer
p.43: Central Press / Stringer
pp.44–45: Mirrorpix
p.49: A. J. O'Brien / Stringer
p.50: Popperfoto
p.51: Popperfoto
p.53: Topical Press Agency / Stringer
p.55: Bert Hardy / Stringer
pp.56–57: Picture Post / Stringer
p.59: Uncredited/AP/Shutterstock
p.61: ANL/Daily Herald/Shutterstock
p.62: ANL/Shutterstock
p.63: Everett/Shutterstock
p.65: Uncredited/AP/Shutterstock
p.67: John Rider-Rider/AP/Shutterstock
p.69: Everett/Shutterstock
p.71: Lichfield
p.72: Tim Graham
p.75: Anwar Hussein
p.76: Anwar Hussein
p.77: Lichfield
p.78(t): Mirrorpix
p.78(b): Hulton Archive / Stringer
p.79: Tim Graham
p.83: - / Getty
p.86: Lisa Sheridan / Stringer
p.87: Hulton Deutsch
p.89: ADRIAN DENNIS / Staff
p.92(t): Mirrorpix
p.92(b): Keystone / Stringer
p.93: Universal History Archive
p.95: Popperfoto
p.99: Universal History Archive
p.108: Shutterstock
p.109: PA Images / Alamy Stock Photo
p.110: PA Images / Alamy Stock Photo
p.111(t): PA Images / Alamy Stock Photo
p.111(b): Paul Popper/Popperfoto
p.112: ADRIAN DENNIS / Stringer
p.113: PA Images / Alamy Stock Photo
p.114: Keystone-France
p.115: Nat Jag
p.117: REUTERS / Alamy Stock Photo
p.118(t): Ken Goff
p.118(b): JOHN STILLWELL / Stringer
p.119: Anwar Hussein

p.122(t): David Levenson
p.122(b): Anwar Hussein
p.123(t): PAUL J. RICHARDS / Staff
p.123(b): WPA Pool / Pool
p.124(t): Bettmann
p.124(b): Georges De Keerle
p.125: Peter Macdiarmid / Staff
p.127: Dan Kitwood / Staff
p.128: RON BELL
p.129(t): UniversalImagesGroup
p.129(b): Rolls Press/Popperfoto
p.130(t): Win McNamee / Staff
p.130(b): Keystone-France
p.131: Popperfoto
p.134(t): Fox Photos / Stringer
p.134(b): PA Images / Alamy Stock Photo
p.135: Anwar Hussein
p.136(t): Anwar Hussein
p.136(b): POOL / Pool
p.137(t): Popperfoto
p.137(b): Popperfoto
p.140: Anwar Hussein
p.141: Anwar Hussein
p.147: Mirrorpix
p.149: THOMAS COEX
p.151: Evening Standard / Stringer
pp.154–155: AFP / Stringer
p.157: Kirstin Sinclair / Stringer
p.158: Anwar Hussein
p.160(l): Shutterstock
p.160(c): Tim Graham
p.160(r): Samir Hussein
p.161(l): Max Mumby/Indigo
p.161(c): Samir Hussein
p.161(r): Tim Graham
p.162(l): David Levenson
p.162(c): Keystone / Stringer
p.162(r): Max Mumby/Indigo
p.163(l): Max Mumby/Indigo
p.163(c): Tim Graham
p.163(r): Samir Hussein
p.164(tl): Reginald Davis/Shutterstock
p.164(tr): Lichfield
p.164(bl): Serge Lemoine / Stringer
p.164(br): Tim Graham
p.165(tl): David Levenson
p.165(tr): Tim Graham
p.165(bl): Ray Bellisario/Popperfoto
p.165(br): Tim Graham
p.166(l): Lisa Sheridan / Stringer
p.166(c): Tim Graham
p.166(r): David Hartley/Shutterstock
p.167(l): Reginald Davis/Shutterstock
p.167(c): ADRIAN DENNIS / Staff
p.167(r): Tim Graham
p.171: Joan Williams/Shutterstock
p.174: Hulton Archive / Stringer
p.175: WPA Pool / Pool
p.176: Lichfield
p.179(t): Lisa Sheridan / Stringer
p.179(b): Central Press / Stringer
p.180(t): PA Images / Alamy Stock Photo

p.180(b): Today/Shutterstock
p.181: Anwar Hussein
p.184: Kirstin Sinclair
p.186: Central Press / Stringer
p.187: Tim Graham
p.188: Peter Macdiarmid / Staff
p.189: Max Mumby/Indigo
p.195: Lisa Sheridan / Stringer
p.196: Tim Graham
p.197: Trinity Mirror / Mirrorpix /
       Alamy Stock Photo
p.199: Lisa Sheridan / Stringer
p.200: Keystone Press / Alamy Stock Photo
p.201(t): Fox Photos / Stringer
p.201(b): Bettmann
p.207: Hulton Deutsch
p.208(t): Anwar Hussein
p.208(b): Central Press / Stringer
p.209: PA Images / Alamy Stock Photo
p.211: Princess Diana Archive / Stringer
p.212: Shutterstock
p.213: JOHN STILLWELL / Staff
p.218: Tim Graham
p.219: Tim Graham
pp.222–223: David Levenson
p.225: REUTERS / Alamy Stock Photo
pp.226–227: JOHN STILLWELL / Staff
p.229: Mark Runnacles / Stringer
p.230(t): Anwar Hussein
p.230(b): WPA Pool / Pool
p.231: PHIL NOBLE / Staff
p.234(t): Max Mumby/Indigo
p.234(bl): Chris Jackson / Staff
p.234(br): John Cantile / Stringer
p.235: Abaca Press / Alamy Stock Photo
p.238(i): Mark Cuthbert
p.238(ii): Max Mumby/Indigo
p.238(iii): Yui Muk/AP/Shutterstock
p.238(iv): Yui Muk/AP/Shutterstock
p.239(i): Robin Utrecht/Shutterstock
p.239(ii): Tim Rooke / Shutterstock
p.239(iii): DAVID HARTLEY/Shutterstock
p.239(iv): Tim Rooke/Shutterstock
p.242(t): Tim Graham
p.242(b): ALASTAIR GRANT / Stringer
p.243(t): UK Press
p.243(b): Mark Cuthbert
p.245: Ray Tang/Shutterstock
p.246(l): Ray Tang/Shutterstock
p.246(r): David Fisher/Shutterstock
p.247: Tim Rooke/Shutterstock
p.252: WPA Pool / Pool
p.253: PA Images / Alamy Stock Photo
p.258: Pool/Max Mumby
p.259: WPA Pool / Pool
p.260: Max Mumby/Indigo
p.261: Max Mumby/Indigo
p.263: WPA Pool / Pool
pp.270–271: Universal History Archive
Hard cover images:
Front: STEVE PARSONS
Back: Lisa Sheridan / Stringer